THE PRIMARY CHURCH SCHOOL

The Primary Church School

HAZEL A. LEWIS

Revised Edition

Published for the
COOPERATIVE PUBLICATION ASSOCIATION
By
THE BETHANY PRESS
St. Louis, Mo.

268. 432
L58p

FOREWORD

Not the least interesting part of revising a book is the discovery of the changes which have taken place since it was first written. In this book which deals with the administrative aspects of the church's work with primary children, the greatest changes are found in the church's emphasis upon the basic responsibility of the home, in more definite working relationships between home and church, and in a greater variety of organizational patterns, as in separation of and combinations of grades. None of these can be said to be universal or even general, but they are definite movements engaging the attention of many church school leaders. They represent ideals toward which many churches are working.

Even more interesting are the basic needs which have not changed, because they are rooted in child nature and in the message of the Christian gospel.

The church is still seeking to make available to children religious experiences which meet their needs. Good teachers, like all good parents, see their work in terms of growing children. It is through what children themselves do, under the guidance of wise parents and teachers, that they will grow in Christian personality, and not through what is done to them.

Therefore any book which deals with organization, administration, planning, supervising must keep ever in its center the needs of children. This is not a theory. It is a fact—an array of facts, which affect equipment, room arrangement, time schedules, personal relationship, all the factors in the provision the church makes for primary children. Learning to live the Christian way is a shared experience, and the great company of parents and church school leaders who join with primary children in this great adventure are finding their own religious experience enriched as they grow in their own capacity for worship, for learning, and for working with others in groups that have Christian ideals and purposes.

The teachers who reviewed the former edition of this book and suggested changes which were desirable, and those who read the revised manuscript and gave constructive criticism, have the deep gratitude of the author.

HAZEL A. LEWIS.

TABLE OF CONTENTS

Chapter IV

Chapter V

Chapter VI

Chapter VII

Chapter I

THE CHURCH AND PRIMARY CHILDREN

PRELIMINARY OBSERVATION

1. Observe a neighborhood group of children. What are the plans and projects they make and carry out together? How do they influence each other?

2. Why do the children you know attend the Primary Department? Is it because of friendship with other children? Is it because they are sent or brought by their parents? How many of them do you think come because it is a matter of personal choice and interest?

3. Discover through informal conversation with the parents of a primary child what they feel the department is doing or should do for their child.

A woman in a certain church was asked to become the superintendent of the Primary Department. Her first question was "What would I be expected to do?" For a moment it was not clear whether she was inquiring about such matters as the amount of time required, the responsibility for maintaining attendance, or other aspects of organization. When asked for an explanation she said, "Oh, I mean, what would I be expected to accomplish and how would I know when I had done it?" The answers to her question led to her acceptance of the responsibility and to many hours of training and study.

The reasons for a Primary Department in terms of what it should accomplish should also answer a parent's question "Why should I send my child to the church school?" Always there must be the fullest realization that what the church does in working directly with children is in no sense a substitute for the religious nurture and teaching of the home. Moreover, the church has the same obligation to help parents that it has to help teachers.

Let us look at some of the reasons why churches carry on the work of teaching children. There are great numbers of ministers and other church leaders who are mindful of the example and words of the Master who "took a child and put him in the midst," on the occasion when the disciples were discussing greatness. They remember that he said "Whoever receives one such child in my name receives me."[1] The spiritual life of the church requires that children shall be included in its fellowship.

This attitude is very different from the motives of the church which provides for children because children are the church of the future. They are, but they are also persons who have needs now. Whatever affects them has meaning in the present even more than in the future. The church that reaches out to bring children into its Sunday and vacation church schools because they will increase the enrollment and may become members of the church some day, is exploiting children for the sake of its own success. Children need to know the love of God now. They need to become acquainted with Jesus, the Friend, now. They are known and loved of God as persons of value. The church must keep its motives sincere in dealing with them. It must feel a genuine concern for the children themselves.

If you were planning the educational work in a church which had never had graded groups for children, what would be your reasons for having a Primary Department, or groups of primary children? Even if there have been graded departments or classes so long that every one takes them for granted it is a good thing occasionally to ask "Why?" and "What is being accomplished?"

WHAT THE CHURCH CAN DO FOR CHILDREN

The church has its own place and function in the religious training of children. There are some things that can be done better by the church, and indeed may not be done at all unless they are done by the church. Let us think about some of these things.

Provide an opportunity for group life. Some of life's adjustments can be made only in the family where old and young help each other and work together in the atmosphere of love. But there are other kinds of learning which take place when children of about the same maturity stimulate each other to discover new ideas and truth, and to develop new skill. When children of about the same age and develop-

[1]Matt. 18:5

ment are given an opportunity to work together they have experiences of learning which they do not have when alone or even in the family group.

Even two children playing and working together are influenced by each other to an extent that makes the total of their thinking and doing much greater than the total of what the two of them would accomplish if each were alone. Every mother can testify that this is true. Each child makes suggestions and is in turn influenced by what other children in a group say and do. All of them furnish ideas and material for their common undertaking. They experience the joy of contributing to the group and receiving the appreciation and approval of the other members. They bring out new ability in one another. Because of this, even children who disagree constantly would rather play together than alone. These experiences contribute to growth in Christian personality and fellowship.

Help each child learn through experiences suited to his own age and development. When children about the same age are grouped together the teaching material and procedures can be suited to their needs. Words, sentences, ideas, experiences can be used with a fair assurance that they will be understood and will help the children in the process of learning and growing. When it is not possible to have a group for each year of age or school grade, the needs are still there and ways must be found to meet them.

Increase the children's contacts with Christian adults. Personal relations with teachers, department leaders, the minister and other church workers have educational value and help children to find their place in the church family. These contacts give opportunity for the children to see Christian faith and ideals exemplified in the lives of these friends.

These are some of the reasons for the church's program for children. Let us look further at the experiences children should have in the Primary Department of the church.

EXPERIENCES THE PRIMARY DEPARTMENT PROVIDES

What are the experiences which are essential to the religious development of children and for which the Primary Department should provide opportunity? As each of these is discovered and analyzed, its significance for the child's individual growth as well as his relationships with others in religious activities, should be considered. The value of "inward compulsion" as against "external compulsion" must be kept in mind as each experience is considered. An experience is valuable to the extent that the children enter into it voluntarily and with interest.

Joining with others in worship. An awareness of God, satisfaction in speaking to God, realization that God speaks to him through the Bible and recognition of opportunities to share in God's work, all come to the child as he joins with other children and the teachers in worship suited to his capacity. His ideas of God are clarified and made more meaningful. Sometimes they are corrected; if, for example, he has acquired a misconception of the nature of God. He may have been afraid of God, thinking of him as one who punished evildoing. He may have looked upon God as a magician who works wonders and bestows or withholds his gifts. These ideas may be corrected by the nature of the prayer and other acts of worship in which he joins with other children, as well as by the discussions with other children under the guidance of a wise and understanding teacher.

If he has had a normal, happy religious experience at home and in the church kindergarten, the conception of God which grew there will be made richer and fuller. Because his knowledge of the world has grown, his appreciation of the goodness of God may grow also. He finds ways of expressing this growing appreciation through the hymns and prayers, and in the work he does.

As he works with God in carrying out plans that he, working with others, has made and that he feels are part of God's plan, he has experiences of joyous companionship that may result in spontaneous worship.

As he learns more of Jesus' life, through story and picture and song, and as he imagines himself having been with Jesus, he has a new and richer understanding of what God is like.

All of this should lead to a desire for a personal relationship with God that finds satisfaction in worship and work.

Discussing and finding answers to religious problems. A primary child's experience in the world has also brought some problems, some of which are sharply defined in his mind, and others which are vague. If he is in a friendly, understanding atmosphere at home and at school, he asks a multitude of questions. These may be answered satisfactorily and conclusively. He may even accept the authority of others as a substitute for his own thinking. On the other hand, his questions may be evaded or answered in ways that are not satisfactory to him. He then seeks information elsewhere, perhaps from sources that are unreliable. A primary child may have problems which he lacks the vocabulary or confidence to express clearly. He faces the age-old problem of good and evil in the world. He sees good people suffering misfortune and sorrow. He wonders how God works in the world. He is unconsciously making for himself a Christian or pagan philosophy of life.

As a member of a group of children, somewhere near his own age, in which he feels free to say what he thinks, he is likely to have his own problems made clear to himself, and to find, in cooperation with other children, satisfactory solutions to some of these problems. Not that he will deliberately sit down to discuss the problems of the universe with a group of other children, but through his contact with them and the experiences of working with them, there will develop the friendly stimulating atmosphere in which questions and opinions come naturally to the surface.

Such conditions as these are likely to be found only where there is the companionship of understanding and helpful adults who share in the experiences and guide them, without imposing their own opinions and views upon the children.

Working with others for worth-while ends. The activities into which children enter whole-heartedly and with the greatest results in learning and character development, are those in which the results are interesting to the children themselves. They are even more valuable when the children discover the need to be met; additionally so when the discovery is made in cooperation with other children and the activity is entered into cooperatively.

A newly appointed primary superintendent found herself in charge of an unattractive room, a group of children who had been described as disorderly, and several teachers who were critical of the children and the equipment, but doing nothing about either. The needs were so immediate and pressing that the longer process of teacher training seemed out of the question for the present. Informal conversation with a few children, who arrived early one Sunday morning, led to the discovery, by the children themselves, of ways in which the room could be rearranged to better advantage, and be made more attractive. As plans were made, the children found their suggestions listened to with respect and they were encouraged to be more thoughtful and original. There were only enough chairs for one seating, though the morning session included work in small groups, and worship when the entire group sat together. The fact was faced by the children and they made plans for the orderly moving of chairs during the session. Teachers joined in the activities as members of the group and found themselves accepted on their own merit. They found themselves eager for additional information and training that might make them more adequate to meet the demands of the situation.

There is always the possibility and danger, with children as well as with adults, that the emphasis in working together will be placed upon energy, thoroughness, and dependability to the exclusion of joyful fellowship and work. The teachers and other adult members of the group can determine this atmosphere by their own attitude toward each other, toward the children, and toward the work in hand. A sense of joy in working together, as well as in the achievements themselves, will be a valuable part of the experience.

Feeling a sense of sharing in God's work. As children find themselves able to achieve desirable and worth-while ends as members of the group, there comes a sense of sharing in God's purposes and working with him that is a more valuable religious experience than can come simply through an awareness of God's goodness and power. As a child finds himself able to achieve, to overcome difficulties, to rise above failures, to rejoice in success, he feels a degree of unity with God that is deep and genuine and so very personal that it sometimes seems quite informal in some of its expressions, but is not irreverent. There comes a sense of responsibility that in turn leads to a new appreciation of God's dependability. The joy of feeling companionship with God in work is a form of worship which for children may be of the utmost value.

Introduction to a widening world. Through the books they are reading, through their school work and in some situations through contact with children of other races, most children have, during their first three years in school, many experiences that broaden their knowledge of the world in which they live and the people who live in it. Sometimes this leads to an emphasis on differences, to a feeling of racial or national superiority. Measured by standards of clothing, customs, living conditions, these differences may seem insurmountable and the child may have a feeling of being shut off from the people of other lands. On the other hand, his interest and curiosity may lead him through the avenues of books, pictures, and personal contact into a sense of world fellowship. Certainly his experiences under the influence of Christian environment and guidance should provide him with ways of entering into friendly relationship with the people of other races. He will discover the ways in which they are unlike and like himself. Perhaps he will meet persons who have traveled in these other lands and who are friends of the people there. Perhaps the missionary whom he meets will be another bond that connects him with the world in which he lives.

Even when the public school provides, as it frequently does, opportunities for establishing international contacts and good will, there is still a responsibility which belongs to the church. The specific task of the Primary Department is to help children realize that the people of the world should be friends because we are all children of one Father.

Having contacts with helpful adults. The contacts between children and grown people are full of possibilities for the development of both. The child who feels that all adults are his enemies, who oppose him in whatever he wishes to do, persons to be endured because they are necessary in certain practical ways, but are quite outside the realm of really interesting and worth-while things, may have had experiences that seem to justify his feeling, but he has a very poor foundation for some of life's most important relationships. On the other hand, the child whose world includes teachers, parents, and other adult friends, whom he admires and imitates, and in whom he has confidence, is likely to find many rich experiences through this relationship. If these adults are wise in their helpfulness, if they respect the personalities of children and if they are fair in their judgments, children have a sense of security which they cannot gain in any other way, and which is essential to their spiritual growth.

Children will not, of course, analyze these relationships. A little boy whose mother said to him, "No wonder you like Miss Brown! She does so many interesting things for you," replied, "No, she doesn't exactly do interesting things, she just lets them happen." Anyone who has worked with boys and girls, six, seven and eight years old, knows how quickly they lose interest in any undertaking when too much assistance is given by solicitous adults and when they find no opportunity for their own initiative. For the sake of winning the approval of the teacher or other adult friend, they may continue their participation in the undertaking, but their attitude is changed. A group of children began with great enthusiasm to plan and arrange an exhibit at the close of a unit of work. Because of her desire that the exhibit would make a good impression on parents and church leaders, the teacher told the children exactly how to do everything. She dominated the situation and the children's joy changed to a plodding sort of effort to get it done in a way that would satisfy the teacher.

There is also the danger that in our anxiety to leave children perfectly free from the domination of adult leaders, we will forget the powerful influence which example has. The child who habitually sees adults who are courteous to each other and to them, who sees teachers and older friends entering with enthusiasm into worth-while projects, who finds them participating in worship with sincerity, desires these same experiences for himself. The experiences are enhanced by the fact that the people whom he admires find value in these same experiences.

Using materials having special religious significance. The glamour of books and pictures and working materials is very great for children in these early years. The contact with these becomes more meaningful when it is shared with other children and when it is part of the larger experiences of living and working together. A beautiful Bible with large print, perhaps with carefully chosen pictures in it, used by the children in connection with their worship experiences or with work they are doing, establishes a relationship which is valuable in their present experience and capable of expansion and enrichment throughout the years. As a child discovers in it stories which he loves, information which he is seeking, and ideas to enjoy, he develops an appreciation which cannot be brought about by a verbal insistence upon its importance.

Some of his deepest feelings, for which he might not himself be able to find words, are interpreted for him and enriched by the music he hears and songs in which he joins with other children. He sees good copies of great paintings and discovers that the great artists about whom he may hear at school or in books were inspired to their greatest work by the same stories from the Bible which he loves.

Creating materials. Perhaps the greatest value of these contacts with materials will not come through the deepening of his appreciation for these things, but through his own creativity inspired by them. He too may write a hymn, paint a picture or the background for a Christmas play; he may write a poem or a story which expresses his religious feeling. Not only is he inspired to creativity by contact with these materials, but by his contact with other children. He finds approval and encouragement in measuring his ability with that of other children his own age. He will probably be a copyist to a certain extent, and strains of other songs, the composition of other pictures, the plots of other stories and the ideas of other poems, will be found in what he does. But he has made these things over into the expression of his own feeling.

Discovering new information and achieving skill. Children delight to achieve, to find out interesting new facts and ways of doing things. Frequently there is satisfaction in the experience of learning, just for its own sake, without any particular appreciation of the result. Children find satisfaction in memorization. For certain types of children there is satisfaction in this tangible sort of achievement. Because of this we are sometimes deceived as to the value of memory work. Certainly no very lasting result in Christian experience will come unless the material that the children memorize has value for them now in their present experiences. When in the course of their worship and work, children arrive at a desire to learn certain things, they will enter into the process with an attitude that will make the achievement, as well as the material learned, of much greater value to them than if the memorization had been imposed. It is reasonable to expect that at some time in connection with their work practically every group of older primary children will become interested in the Bible as a book, and in discovering a few simple facts about it, such as where to find certain treasured stories or passages. Intensive study of this sort, however, is better suited to the Junior Department.

Primary children have certain new skills of which they are very proud. They are beginning to read, and to write a little, and to count. It is not the business of the church school to teach any of these subjects, but the learning experiences of the children in the church school will be more meaningful if these skills, as far as the children possess them, are used. Contact with simple Bible story books, assistance with certain vocabulary difficulties because of the unfamiliarity of words that they do not meet in their schoolbooks, the doing of such writing as is within their ability, the caring for materials involving the skill of counting and making lists, all make use of the ability which the children have. The teacher who ignores the children's abilities along these lines and proceeds as though they were not able to do any of these things, loses a large amount of co-operation that would otherwise be available.

The most valuable skill which we may hope that the children will acquire through their contact with other children and with adult leaders in the Primary Department, will be skill in living and working with other people. Discovering satisfaction in making a contribution to common tasks and in accepting the contribution of others, in sharing working materials, in giving up one's own way that the greater good may be accomplished, in exercising self-control when to do otherwise would spoil the happy time and the good work, leads to ideas and attitudes that are essential to Christian living.

A group of children who painted the background scene for a Christmas service that they had planned, acquired in connection with the undertaking a considerable amount of knowledge that they did not have before, including information about oriental customs, passages from the Bible, hymns, and great pictures. They also acquired in the process increased skill in working together and satisfaction in the fellowship of work.

INDIVIDUAL GROWTH

The various experiences which have just been described and for which the church may provide opportunity, have been described in terms of children as members of a group. Yet results must be measured by the experience of the individual child, for the most satisfactory group experience is not valuable in itself no matter how successful the work of the group may seem to be, either in process or in result. It is what happens to individual children that determines whether or not the experience is valuable. In each of the experiences described, the significance of it for individual growth will be quite apparent.

The experience of joining with others in worship will be valuable if it results in an increased awareness of God, a clearer understanding of how God works, and a deepened joy and satisfaction in the relationships expressed through worship. This is a deeply personal matter. The result is not to be found in an orderly beautiful worship service, but in the changes in attitude and knowledge which have come to individual children.

The most valuable result of the discussions by the children of their own religious problems will be found not only in the answers which they discover, but also, and sometimes primarily, in that attitude toward the seeking for truth which an individual child acquires. The experience of working with others for worth-while ends will be valuable not only in the ends accomplished but in the joy of fellowship which becomes part of the child's way of living. The same significance for individual growth will be found in each of the other five group experiences described. They will vary according to the needs and interests of the individual children, but they will succeed or fail according to the changes that have been wrought in the children themselves.

It must also be remembered that while the foregoing experiences have been described in terms of desirable situations and outcomes, they are all capable of providing undesirable and harmful experiences. The other side of the picture may be found in connection with each one of them. Children may get wrong ideas of God, they may find wrong answers to their religious problems or become fixed in those already acquired, they may have unhappy experiences in working with others, and become selfish rather than co-operative, and so on through all of the experiences which may come to them in their contact with other primary children and with the adult leaders.

TWO PRIMARY DEPARTMENTS

Let us visit the Primary Departments in two churches.

The Primary room in the first church was well situated and furnished. The walls were a delicate shade, the wood-work was painted ivory, the carpet was beautiful, the furniture was of mahogany.

Two beautiful pictures, copies of masterpieces, were gifts in memory of a former superintendent and of a child who had died. The donors had asked the present superintendent what pictures she wanted and these had been highly recommended in a book.

The supplies (papers, construction materials, etc.) were kept in a fine cabinet and the secretary gave them to the teachers who called at her desk before they went to their classes.

The superintendent had a carefully planned program of songs, Scripture responses, prayer (the children joined in a prayer poem), a story, and an announcement of a service project in which the department was to join. The reason for their sharing was stated thus by the superintendent, "I told them I knew the Primary Department would want to do its part. I can always count on my teachers and children to do their full share of anything I ask them to do." (Teachers nodded approvingly, children looked rather pleased that they were evidently doing the right thing.) "Now, next Sunday each one of you is to bring—" and the details of the plan were revealed to them.

The classes went to their rooms in orderly fashion, records were made out and collected by the secretary, who also distributed the papers at the right time. When the classes reassembled, memory verses were recited, the children were reminded of what they were to bring the next Sunday, and the session closed with a song and a prayer in unison.

Someone may say, "Surely planned programs and orderliness are not out of date and frowned upon!" Not unless they are the result of "external compulsion." The situation just described is an accurate picture of a department provided *for* Primary children.

The Primary room in the second church would appear at first glance to be less orderly than the first. There were many things in addition to the height of the chairs to indicate it was a children's room. On a low easel near the front of the room a lovely picture had been placed by some children who had chosen it. The table at the front gave evidence of arrangement by children's hands. Flowers had been placed in different parts of the room by children. Children were getting working materials, books, and other things from the cabinet. Groups were at work in various parts of the room. The superintendent and a group of children were gathered informally around the piano, choosing songs and other materials for the program. The superintendent's plan for the session had included sufficient material that there was room for choice by the children. She guided and shared in the discussions that led to the selections.

Music called the groups from their varied activities and they assembled for a period of fellowship and worship. The children had things to report, work to share, questions to ask. Plans for further work were made.

One group had discovered a need that was greater than they could care for alone and asked the rest of the children to help. A family of children who were quarantined and whose father was out of work needed games, pictures, and stories to keep them happy while they had to stay in the house. It was agreed that these things should be the sort that could be burned when the time of quarantine was over. Grown people were taking food and coal to the family, but children would know best how to make things that other children would enjoy. The ages of the children and their interests were discussed, and plans made for beginning that very week to send them a package of homemade games, stories from their papers, picture books made of heavy wrapping paper. More than half the suggestions came from the children, as well as the problems that should be considered.

When the plans were fairly well made, the enthusiasm of the children found expression in the song "There's work in the world for the children to do,"[2] and the children were ready and eager to talk to God. The superintendent read quietly from the Bible a passage which deepened the satisfaction of working with God. Other songs and the offering had their natural place in the program. The children returned to the small groups where they had been at work and the unit of work for each grade was carried on. In some cases the project which had been planned was used in the small group and in others was put aside momentarily for other work they had in hand.

When the groups returned they shared a variety of things with each other. Some were Bible verses, some told of work they were doing, and one group told of their plans for participating in the project planned earlier in the session. This served to remind the others of what they were planning to do.

The first department described was *for* primary children. The second was a department *of* primary children. The room, furnishings, adult leaders, were provided by the church as an opportunity for learning, but one which must be used by the children if it was to be of any real value to them.

The second session was as orderly as the first but it was the orderliness of purposeful activity. It had been planned as carefully as the first program, for all of the apparently spontaneous situations had been in the mind of the leader, although the exact form they would take had been left for the children and the occasion to determine. A free, stimulating environment and sympathetic companionship had been provided.

This description of both of these Primary Departments could be translated into terms of a small group meeting in a one-room church building. There is always the opportunity for creating a teaching situation in which the children share the responsibility and work, wherever there are children and an understanding adult leader. The time available and the equipment may limit the program in some ways but need not change its character greatly.

---

[2] *Worship and Conduct Songs*, Shields.

The differences between the two sessions will be found in skillful administration and teaching. The purpose of any study of administration must be the discovery of ways to provide opportunity for such desirable experiences as will result in the greatest possible religious growth for each child.

SUGGESTIONS FOR FURTHER STUDY AND DISCUSSION

1. Discover the reasons held by church leaders, parents, teachers, for the importance of the church's work with primary children.

2. Plan a session, or part of one, for a Primary Department, which would provide opportunities for worship, fellowship, and creative planning by children. Indicate what your part as an adult member of the group would be and what growth in the children's religious attitudes or conduct you would look for. Keep this plan for reference later as you study further the administration of the Primary Department.

3. Recall situations in which the children had some of the experiences described in this chapter. What provided the opportunity? To what extent did it come from the interest of the children? How could it have been more valuable to the children?

4. Analyze the two Primary Departments described on the three preceding pages and list the ways in which the second one provided greater opportunity for learning and for Christian growth.

Chapter II

GROUPING AND ORGANIZATION

PRELIMINARY OBSERVATION

1. Observe the effect which older and younger children have on each other when engaged in work or play; the attitudes of boys and girls toward each other. If possible observe these in neighborhood play groups, and at school, as well as in church school.

2. Find out through informal conversation with children six to eight years of age the groups they enjoy most and why.

———————

Organization is for the purpose of getting persons and things in right relations to each other so that certain work may be done and certain ends achieved. The success of the organization of the Primary Department of a church is measured by the extent to which children are learning and growing in ways that are Christian. The organization may take any one of a variety of forms according to the number of children to be taught, the space and time available, the workers who can be found, the grouping for which the curriculum is planned. But basically the organization, the curriculum, the teachers exist to meet the needs of children and should be thought of in relation to children.

It seems fair to say that the trend in church schools as well as in general education, is to organize personnel, equipment, materials, in terms of children's learning, rather than simply for administrative efficiency.

For example, in the matter of attendance records, there is a growing tendency to see in them a direct relation to the children's development and not simply a record of average attendance, which can be very misleading if during the year there are two or three special days with high attendance. Rather the records are used to study individual children, to discover the causes of irregular attendance, or the lack of continuity in the work of classes and departments. It is the record of a child that is significant, not the school's record.

THE WHOLE PROGRAM FOR PRIMARY CHILDREN

Any consideration of organization for the religious education of primary children must include more than the session of the church school. The title of this book implies a belief that such a plan of organization must take into account everything which the church provides, directly or indirectly, for primary children. There may be other organizations or sessions within the church which include primary children such as a Church School of Missions, or a family night; there may be a vacation church school or weekday church school conducted by the church or one in which it participates. If so, the church through its education board or committee faces the problem of making it possible for all of these agencies or organizations to work together in providing adequate opportunities for the religious growth of primary children, without undesirable duplications and without the omission of essential factors. The primary leaders may be the ones who will call to the attention of the church leaders the need for facing this problem. The leaders in each of the groups which include primary children may be asked to meet with a representative of the education committee or board to plan together. These persons might constitute a Primary Council, which would study the needs of the children and plan together to meet these needs through the available sessions and through a carefully planned curriculum. The addition of two or three parents with educational vision would be valuable. Such a council might consider whether all the organizations are necessary and helpful, and make recommendations to the education board concerning their continuance.

All of the children, leaders, activities, sessions, and material would then constitute "The Primary School of the Church," even though it were not advisable to drop the names attached to different sessions or groups within the organization. Unity of purpose is more important than uniformity in organization.

Whenever the term "Primary Department" is used in this book it is not to be construed as referring only to the Sunday morning session. It is used for convenience as being more inclusive than "group" or "organization."

This inclusive organization for primary children must of course be consistent with the plan of organization for all the children's departments although there may be variations within the general plan. As was said above, this should be determined first of all in the light of the children's needs and the experiences for which we hope to provide opportunity. But there are other factors that will have to be taken into account in each local situation. These should be studied from two angles; what is now available and what addition or change is needed.

Obviously a church which has only ten primary children, a screened corner for a meeting place, an hour's session on Sunday, and one primary teacher, would plan a very different organization from one that would be suitable where there are a hundred children, a separate room, a Sunday session and a vacation school, two leaders, and a staff of ten teachers. But it may also be true that the first church could find other children to bring into its primary group, could build a room or find one near by, could secure additional leaders, and extend its time on Sunday or into the week day; and that the second church could improve its organization, find additional rooms, improve its leadership, and give its children greater opportunity for practice in Christian living.

TYPES OF ORGANIZATION

The Primary Department usually consists of children six, seven, and eight years of age and in the first three grades of the public school. Variations from this will be discussed later. Some of the plans for organization are discussed here.

1. **The department plan.** In this, which is the one most commonly found, the children of the three primary grades meet in one group for worship and fellowship, and in small groups, one or more for each grade, for work and study. The number in each group may vary from six to twelve depending upon the size of the space available, the skill of the teacher, and the length of time available.

This plan will require a department superintendent, assistants, secretary, pianist, and a teacher for each group of children, with associate or assistant teachers. The needs and limitations of the situation will determine the number of workers required. For example, in a certain church there were thirty children in one fairly large room. One of the three teachers was a good pianist; a girl who was a teacher in training was the secretary; another girl who had some training in Primary work was a substitute teacher; and on the rare occasions when more than one substitute was required, the department superintendent used this as an opportunity for first-hand experience in a teaching situation. The two student teachers assumed major responsibility for work done in part of the expanded session. Thus a staff of six persons carried a fairly comprehensive program of work. Sometimes this is called the group graded plan, especially if the children are all using the same lesson material and are grouped according to interests for work and study.

2. **The two-grade department.** There is a growing tendency to organize departments with a narrower age range. Every primary worker knows the many problems that arise in trying to provide for children just entering first grade and those who have reached the lofty heights of the third grade. It can be done but there are always compromises.

The usual two-grade grouping is first and second grades, third and fourth grades, fifth and sixth grades. These departments are sometimes called: Primary, Lower Junior, and Junior; or Primary, Primary High, and Junior; or Primary I, Primary II, and Junior.

When numbers are not large, the Lower-Upper Junior combinations may meet together for fellowship and various types of activities and have separate class group experiences.

Working out this plan is a matter for study by the workers involved, especially the primary and junior, and by the education committee. It calls for adjustments in the use of space and equipment, which will be considered in the next chapter.

3. **The single-grade unit.** In this plan children of one grade constitute one group, with their own room, teacher, and assistants. All work and worship are carried on apart from other grades, except when inter-group activities arise. If there are more than thirty children, there should be more than one group. Twenty makes a more desirable group in each grade, measured by the opportunity for the participation of every child. The length of the session would also affect the number desirable, for the shorter the time, the greater the problem in creating a natural situation in which all the group participate freely.

In any case, there should be a teacher and assistant for twenty children or less, a teacher and two assistants if the group is between twenty and thirty.

4. The single class in the small school. The age range should not be too wide, nor the group larger than the skill of the teacher and the equipment make advisable. It is often possible to have first and second grade children in one class, third and fourth grades in another, fifth and sixth in another, carrying out the two-grade plan in three classes. This requires three classes instead of two, but makes it possible to meet the needs of children more effectively.

The child who is one of six or eight in the primary class of a small church has the same spiritual needs as the child who is one of eighty children in a large church. His church must see that those needs are met through Christian teaching.

PLACING CHILDREN IN THE RIGHT GROUP

Children usually come into the Primary Department in one of two ways. They are either promoted as a group at a certain time from the Kindergarten Department or they are brought by parents or friends and enrolled at some time during the year. When they are promoted from the Kindergarten Department they are usually about six years of age and are in or will soon enter the first grade in the public school. They constitute the first grade of the Primary Department. However, there may be a larger number than can be included in one group and there must be some basis for determining how they will be divided. The month of birth may be used if age is the basis for grading, or the school semester if public school grade is the basis. Better still is a study of the children to discover the best working groups. The problem is slightly different for the child who enters irregularly during the year, but it is just as important that he should be placed in the right group.

The department leader and the first grade teachers should have opportunity for establishing friendly relationships with the children before they come from the Kindergarten Department. The Kindergarten teacher may have a party and include the primary leaders. Or, the primary leader may go into the kindergarten room to be introduced as a new friend who will be looking for the children who will be promoted to the Primary Department. Better still, there may be such friendly inter-group activities that the kindergarten and primary leaders and children come to know each other long before the time of promotion.

There is always a danger that a system of grading will be relied upon too rigidly and that individual children will not be studied sufficiently. Yet a child's attitude toward the church and toward religion may be profoundly affected by the group in which he is placed, and by the first hour that he spends in the Primary Department. "The opening day of school in the first grade is a day of pupil adjustment. It is not the teacher's day, it is the child's day."[1]

Too often in the church school there is the impression that the person who is enrolling the child is chiefly interested in maintaining the system of grading. It is of the utmost importance that the child shall feel that he has met a friend who is interested in him and is trying to help him find the very best possible place. The art of the child interview is nowhere more needed than in this first contact between the child and the Primary Department. Purposes will probably be served best through friendly conversation rather than through direct personal questions. The department superintendent, or the supervisor, or the department secretary may be the person best fitted to do this.

One wise and understanding department superintendent took the child (or group of children) on a tour of the department room, pointed out the various classes and explained the activities that were carried on in the room so that the child might see the department as a whole before he became part of it. Then in an informal and friendly conversation she discovered something of his previous experience in the church school, his public school grade and his general attitude toward a great many things. But in any case the mechanical operation of filling out an enrollment card with the child's name and address, birthday, telephone number, grade at school, parents' name, was done after the friendly relationship had been established and was made to seem of secondary importance. Efficiency need not be sacrificed, but neither should

[1]Stormzand and McKee, *The Progressive Primary Teacher*, page 75. Houghton Mifflin Company. Used by permission.

friendly good will suffer because of it. The time required to get a child properly launched in his new relationship is not lost.

Age or public school grade. Which shall be used as the basis for grouping children in the Primary Department? Certainly both should be taken into account. If the first grade of the Primary Department consists of children who are six years old, or who will be by a certain date after the beginning of the church school year, most of the children will probably be in the first grade of the public school or will enter it during the year. Children who are seven years of age will probably be in the second grade of the public school, and those who are eight years old in the third grade. These would quite naturally constitute the first, second, and third grades of the Primary Department in the church. But there will always be exceptions. For example, a seven-year-old child may be unusually advanced and in the third grade of the public school, while another one may have been retarded and be in only the first grade. Wherever possible, exceptions of this sort should be made a matter of conference between the parents and the church school leader.

Many leaders have found that they seem to get the most normal grouping of the children by using public school grade as a basis and making exceptions when the child is above the age for that grade, but not when he is below the age, unless their observation of the child and conference with his parents make it evident that this is desirable. The same results could be achieved if age were used as the basis and exceptions were made according to the public school grade. It must be kept in mind that the objective is to have each child in the group where he will be most likely to have desirable experiences.

Individual development and variation. Even within groups that have the same age and public school grade there are differences that must be taken into account, if there is to be more than one group for that age and grade. The practice of the public school in the community may be a guide in this respect, although it should not be followed too closely. But if children who are slow in thinking, in reaching decisions, in expressing their opinions or in muscular skill, are placed with children who are quick in all of these matters, the slower children are likely to have fewer opportunities to contribute to the work of the group and often acquire a sense of inferiority. On the other hand, the child who makes the more rapid progress may gain too good an opinion of his own ability or become discouraged if he is held back by the slower members of the group. If the primary superintendent will observe the children who are to be promoted from the Kindergarten Department and will confer with the superintendent of that department, she will usually discover certain individual differences which will help her to group the children to their best advantage. Groups may be adjusted from year to year, or even during a year, when it seems desirable. No system of grading will work automatically or take the place of a sympathetic understanding of the children themselves as individuals.

In the single-grade plan of organization or in the group graded plan, the adjustments between these children of different types may be made naturally in the development of the small interest groups. The very differences may create situations which are valuable opportunities for learning, and will result in tolerance and helpfulness, especially in longer sessions, as in vacation school.

Boys and girls grouped together. A more normal situation is usually created when boys and girls are grouped together, since they are accustomed to being together in the public school, in the home, and in most neighborhood play groups. When there is an antagonism between boys and girls, it is usually the reflection of things that have been said by older children or by adults and should be overcome by setting up normal situations in which boys and girls work together. However, the plan or organization should be sufficiently flexible so that, when it is desirable for a group of boys or of girls to work separately in a particular activity, the arrangement will be possible. Such occasions will probably be very rare.

PROMOTION

The last Sunday in September has been the usual date of Promotion Day in the church school. This came into general use when graded lessons were first planned. It was felt that children should begin their work in the new grade in the church school at about the time they entered a new grade in public school, and the graded lessons are planned to parallel the school grade, with the summer quarters rounding out the year's work.

There are situations in which the workers feel it is desirable to promote children to the next grade or department in June at about the time they complete a public school grade. There is a feeling that this satisfaction in achievement and in getting ahead should be felt in the church school at the same time. When a church has a different schedule and organization for the summer, or is closed during the summer months, the June promotion is logical.

There are problems connected with either date. When a child is promoted from the third grade in public school, he says "I'm in the fourth grade now." He should feel that his church friends recognize his progress and share his satisfaction in it. Yet he will not actually be in the fourth grade until the next fall. The church school is a year-round school and children can understand that this makes a difference.

When children enter a new grade or department the first of July they are doing so at a time when the attendance of teachers and children is frequently irregular and the new children may not become well integrated into the fellowship and work of the new department. The situation is particularly marked in the Primary Department. If children come in June from the Kindergarten Department they will have made none of the adjustments which take place in public school. They are not prepared to participate in the department activities with children who have completed first and second grades.

Adjustments must be made in the use of most lesson courses if promotion takes place in June. The printed materials for the teacher usually give suggestions. Units may be selected for the summer months from the year's work prepared for that grade or year. The workers in the departments involved should plan together a summer curriculum which will take full advantage of the children's additional free time.

The time of promotion should be decided upon the basis of the greatest value for the children's development through their church school experience.

RELATIONSHIPS

While children should be grouped in grades for the sake of the best opportunities for learning, there must also be opportunities for inter-group and inter-departmental activities. These will frequently arise in connection with work being done in the different classes. Sometimes they will develop as part of the department activity.

A group of primary children who had greatly enjoyed a Christmas scene that they had arranged, invited the kindergarten children to join them one Sunday morning. They chose songs which they thought the younger children would enjoy and in which they could join, and made plans for the comfort and happiness of their guests. In turn they were received in the Kindergarten Department on another occasion and while they accepted the invitation with a little condescension from the superior height of their advanced years, they had a very good time and an experience in the graciousness of receiving as well as giving. A group discovered a need in the Nursery Class and in cooperation with the teacher in that group they provided a number of things for the children.

It is not as easy to arrange helpful contact between groups of adults and children, but it should be done. One group of primary children made lovely Easter greetings for all the members of the Woman's Bible Class, keeping it a great secret. The experience of interchange was made complete when some of the women from the class visited them on Easter Sunday and brought them a lovely plant for the primary room, which the children later shared with a grown-up friend who was ill. The more spontaneous these experiences can be, the more valuable they are.

The children need also a sense of being a part of the whole church. In connection with their class work children in larger churches will probably visit different parts of the church building, the sanctuary, the church office and the pastor's study. There should be opportunities for friendly contact with the pastor, the superintendent of the school, and the director of religious education, as well as other officers and persons connected with the life and work of the church. When these contacts can come naturally in connection with activities that are going on, they become a more vital part of the children's experience than when they are formally arranged for, although the contact should be made whether it arises naturally or not.

A group of primary children who had a party in their room on Saturday afternoon realized how much additional work this made for the janitor and helped him all they could before they left. When they came on Sunday morning and found their room in perfect order, they were filled with delight and amazement. Those who came first rushed off to tell the janitor how good he was to take care of their room, and later in the session a formal message of appreciation was planned and sent to him.

Contacts with groups outside their own church will also be part of children's experience in a widening world. The teachers and the department superintendent will work together in making these experiences possible and helpful.

No discussion of organization or relationships would be complete without a consideration of the close relationship that should exist between the teacher and the members of her group. There is always the question as to whether the teacher should progress with her class, being promoted with them from year to year, or should specialize in one grade receiving a new group of pupils each year. The advantage of the teacher going on with her class is that of longer and more intimate acquaintance resulting in a better knowledge of the children. There is a disadvantage, however, that the contacts of the children will be more limited, the teacher will be unable to become as skillful in handling a particular grade, and the children will have had the advantage of the understanding and enrichment of only one teacher throughout their experience in the Primary Department. A teacher who followed a group of children throughout the department said that after she had become accustomed to the vocabulary and capacity of third-grade children she found that it required considerable time for her to become accustomed again to the limitations of first-grade children. Other things being equal, it is probably best for primary children to have each year a teacher who is experienced and skillful in that particular grade. Of course there is no rule in a matter of this kind. The needs of the children in a particular situation must be the basis of the plan to be followed.

SUGGESTIONS FOR FURTHER STUDY AND DISCUSSION

1. Study the building in which your church school meets, the available leadership, and discover whether or not the present form of organization could be modified to the advantage of the primary work.

2. Plan for an interview with a new child who is entering the Primary Department, either an imaginary experience or a real one if there is opportunity. Discover the possibility of such an interview in establishing friendly relationship with the child and in placing him properly in the department. What improvement would you suggest in the method of enrollment used in your church school?

3. Plan what you would consider an ideal form of organization for ten, thirty, fifty, or one hundred children, according to the situation with which you are most familiar. Take into account the factors in the local situation, decide which of the five forms of organization would seem best suited, and plan the grouping of the children and the necessary staff of workers.

Chapter III

HOME AND CHURCH RELATIONSHIPS

PRELIMINARY OBSERVATION

1. Discuss with several parents the needs of their children which they think religion should help to meet, the part they feel the home must do, and the help they feel the church should give them.

2. Why, in your opinion, do parents send their children to the Primary Department? Make a list of the reasons.

3. At what points in the program of the Primary Department does co-operation between the parents and the primary workers seem to be most necessary or at what points does it break down because of lack of co-operation?

THE FIRST RESPONSIBILITY

Unquestionably the religious education of children is the responsibility of their parents. No institution outside the home, not even the church, can relieve them of that responsibility although it may help to perform it. The church also has a responsibility to the children just as it has to the grown people who are members of its community. When parents send their children to the church school, tacitly they are saying, "We would like to share this responsibility with you." Unfortunately they are sometimes saying, "We do not know anything about teaching religion. Will you please take care of it for us?" And that is just what the church cannot do.

There is no greater compliment that can be paid to a group of workers in the church school than when parents trust them to teach religion to their children. Sometimes church school leaders feel that parents should be very grateful to the volunteer or professional workers who dedicate so much of their lives to the religious instruction of their children, but it is equally true that teachers of children should have a sense of profound gratitude for the high honor and privilege which fathers and mothers give when they bring their children to the church to be taught. The leader who does not feel a thrill of satisfaction as well as a deep sense of responsibility, when a mother places her small son's hand in that of the teacher, either figuratively or literally, and says by that act, "Teach him, be his friend and guide," has not tasted the spiritual joy of being a teacher. It is easy to become mechanical, to take things for granted, to look upon a child as just one more enrolment for the department and so to lose, or perhaps never to have, a sense of comradeship with parents in the nurture and training of children.

Perhaps the child just strays into the department or is brought by a child friend or by church visitors who are zealous to build up the school, and the parents scarcely know where he is, except to feel sure that he is being well cared for. Then the responsibility for stimulating the interest of the parents rests with the church school worker. A brief period once a week will not go very far in making religion a vital factor in a child's life unless there is a corresponding interest on the part of those who influence his life as profoundly as his parents do.

ESTABLISHING WORKING RELATIONSHIPS

With interested church families. Before the workers in a Primary Department begin making plans for home contacts it is important to find out the other church relationships the parents maintain. If they are active members of the church where their children attend they will probably have responsibilities in one or more committees or organizations of the church. They will be found in meetings of these groups. Sometimes the best approach to them will be through these channels. For example, in one church there is a young adult class of which nearly all the parents of primary children are members. Many of the matters which are the mutual concern of parents and teachers become part of the program of that class. The teachers are guests at one of the class meetings each year. The teachers go to the leaders for counsel and to bring information about the work of the Primary Department.

In some churches there is a class or fellowship for the cultivation of Christian family life. That is a natural point of contact for teachers of children.

None of these takes the place of personal relationships with the parents of the children in the Primary Department in ways which will be discussed later in this chapter.

With non-church families. In many churches the number of children who come from non-church families are a considerable proportion of the enrolment. Whether there are two or twenty such families, they present a different situation from that found in church families. Add to these the families whose connection with the church is only nominal, who are indifferent toward the church and religion, and the percentage is higher than is sometimes realized. There is sometimes a tendency to be aware of two or three typical families and think that these represent the whole picture. Nothing but an analysis of the church relationships of the families of all the children in a department will reveal the actual situation.

When parents and teachers are working together for the Christian nurture of children far more can be accomplished than if they worked separately. But to say that nothing can be achieved by the church unless the home is also actively concerned is not true. The law of contrast operates in some cases. A child from an irreligious home who finds love, order, beauty, purposefulness, in the church may respond to God's love and choose the Christian way of life. This does not mean that he will turn against his parents or cease to love them, but that he will choose a better way for himself because of the Christian influence provided by the church.

The greater problem exists when the home is good in every material sense of comfort and family love, but without concern for spiritual things or knowledge of religion. In these situations as well as in the case of the non-church home, relationships must be set up through direct contact between a child's teachers and his parents. Under these conditions it is well to work in cooperation with the minister and the Adult Department of the church. The best way to help a child is through his parents and if the workers in a young adult class succeed in bringing them into a closer relationship with church life, the way will be open for closer cooperation in the child's religious nurture. Besides, this contact with parents who send their children to the church school offers one of the most fruitful evangelistic opportunities.

Frequently the first step is for the primary workers to discover the church relationship, or lack of it, of the parents of each child in the department.

For the purpose of analyzing the facts (not of classifying persons for that is as undesirable as it is impossible) some such listing may be made as: 1) children of parents having active connection with the church; 2) children of parents having only nominal membership in the church; 3) children of parents having no connection with the church. There are usually children who for some reason are being cared for by persons other than their parents or who come from broken homes. The church school teacher must be aware of this. Nothing hurts a child more than to have some one refer to his mother or father when he has none.

THE CHURCH PROGRAM FOR PARENTS

The family is the unit of the church far more than a class or department in the school can be. Sermons that challenge parents, community, activities that interest and help parents, classes in which they may study their problems and discuss them, courses of lectures, books and other literature, are all means that the church may use in a program of parent education. A large part of such a program may be carried on through the Adult Department of the church school. Through the departmental organizations, through special classes and in other ways this department may be providing parents with guidance and inspiration. It is not the function of the Primary Department, any more than that of any other, to see that a complete program of parent education is set up within the church. The leaders in the department may call the attention of the Education Committee or other church leaders to the need for parent education and cooperate fully in carrying it out. If nothing is being done and there seems to be no possibility of a church program for parents, the leaders in the Primary Department, perhaps in cooperation with the other children's departments, may need to go further in providing help for parents. There are, moreover, certain forms of specific cooperation for which the Primary Department workers are directly responsible. The Education Committee can be of great service in unifying all of these efforts and making sure that there are no duplications nor serious omissions.

Whatever the program of parent education may be in the local church, the primary teacher and leader can never forget the fact that the religious and social ideals of the parents constitute the greatest aid or the greatest hindrance to the religious education of the children in their classes. Parents who have strong racial prejudice can completely nullify, in the course of conversation in the home, all effort toward missionary education and social adjustment for the children. The conceptions of religion which parents have are felt by the children even when they are not fully understood. A conversation that is overheard or a thoughtless statement made to a child may confuse him and sometimes counteract the most carefully planned program of religious education.

On the other hand, the parents who have religious faith themselves, who do not try to force their religious ideas upon the children but simply to share them, who have a sympathetic knowledge of child nature, will increase the effectiveness of the work in the church school immeasurably, by their attitudes, their conversation, and by their definite effort to guide and enrich the children's religious experience. Such parents are not simply cooperating with the church school; they are providing for the religious education of their children, in which the work of the church school is one contributing factor.

In any consideration of the relationship between parents and school it must be kept in mind that in most churches the parents themselves are part of the teaching staff of the school. Perhaps the mother became interested through her own child, or it may be that fathers and mothers in the church have felt so keenly the responsibility for the teaching of children that they have been willing and anxious to share in that task. There are, therefore, many individuals in the church who have the twofold relationship of parent-teacher, although they are usually not the teachers of their own children.

DIRECT CONTACT WITH PARENTS

Social relationships. It is fortunate when conditions in the church and community are such that the teachers of children in the church are also part of the social life which includes the parents of the children. Sometimes the distances at which the church members live makes this very difficult. But for her own sake as well as for the sake of her work with the children, the teacher should seek opportunities for contacts with parents and other church leaders, through the

social meetings of the Adult Department and the general
social life of the church. A teacher must be a successful
human being if he or she is to be a good teacher.

Personal contact. No amount of organization, no schedule
for calling in the homes of the children, will ever take the
place of a genuinely friendly relationship between parents
and teachers. If Mrs. B. is merely a name on a card with a
certain address and telephone number, who should be seen
because her small son is a problem in the Primary Department, Mrs. B. will be fully aware that she is that and no
more. If the church has no other contact with her than the
fact that her child is in the Primary Department that will of
course be the basis for the first approach. But if she can feel
that she is appreciated as a person and that the department
superintendent or teacher who calls is not doing so perfunc-
torily, she and the teacher will come to a much better understanding and be able to help each other in their common responsibility, which is the religious education of Mrs. B's little
boy.

Calling requires great tact. It is not a social custom any
longer in many communities and when people call without a
previous social engagement to do so, they are usually looked
upon as having something to sell or to promote. If the
teacher and the mother are not personally acquainted, it is a
good plan to arrange for the first call by a telephone conversation or a note. This gives the mother, who may be a
busy woman, an opportunity to appear to better advantage
in the first contact. If the mother and the teacher are acquainted in other relationships, the teacher may approach
this first call by saying some day when they meet, "I have
some problems connected with my work in the Primary Department that I wish I could talk over with you some day.
When would be a convenient time for me to call?" Perhaps
the mother will jump to the conclusion that her child is one
of the "problems." But if she soon discovers that the teacher's attitude is entirely sympathetic and not critical, and that
she does not look upon any child as a problem but as an opportunity, she will be glad to talk with her. Or perhaps the
mother and teacher do not know each other very well. The
teacher may say, "I am John's teacher now and I am eager
to get better acquainted with his mother." In these extremely

busy modern times the telephone has largely taken the place of a personal call. Perhaps it will sometimes have to serve as a contact between the teacher and mother, but it is too bad when this is so for there are certain qualities of friendship that can be achieved only in face-to-face conversation.

Prearranged interviews. There are schools which arrange regularly for a personal interview between the parents and the church school leader. One school makes the request of the parents when the child is enrolled in the school. They are asked to come to the department in which the child is enrolled, at least once a year, to visit the department and to have an interview with the department superintendent. She discusses with them the objectives toward which they are working, the progress that the child is making, and together they face the success and failures of the work which is being done in the department. The superintendent listens courteously and eagerly to the questions and criticisms offered by the parents. She places before them very frankly the situation as the workers in the Primary Department see it. Perhaps she arranges for an interview later between the teacher and the parents.

Parents visiting the department. Anyone who has seen the look of pride with which a child brings his mother or father to the Primary Department knows what a bond of sympathy may be established between the church and the home by this simple fact of the parent's presence in the department. Since parents are busy and may not be sure that they will be entirely welcome, the department superintendent and teachers may take the initiative in inviting the parents to come. The situation will be more normal if all parents do not come on one day, except for some special occasion. The children in a class may invite their parents when they have completed a unit of work or a special project and have an exhibit to share with them. One department sent invitations to seven or eight parents for each month in the year, sending second and third invitations to those who were not able to come in response to the first. The children should have the opportunity to act as hosts when their parents come, to show them about the room, to introduce them to teachers and other friends and to have the parents remain with them during the class and assembly period, if they so desire. Or perhaps some special place will be provided for them to sit and they will join the class group informally. At some time during the visit the department superintendent should have the opportunity to talk with them concerning the work of the department and to receive suggestions and problems.

Parents' Council. A group of parents who are particularly interested in the work of the Primary Department may be appointed as a Parents' Council or Advisory Committee to confer with the workers in the department and to help to reach the other parents who have children there. One mother calling on another mother in the interest of the Primary Department will frequently discover situations and needs which a church school worker had not been able to find. Such a committee can be very outspoken in its challenge to other parents because they themselves are setting the example of their own interest and active cooperation. A Parents' Committee should be appointed, or at least approved by the Education Committee, although the primary superintendent and teachers may request the appointment of it and are in a position to indicate who would be the most interested and active. Invitations to parents' meetings are issued in cooperation with or in the name of such a committee. The supply of equipment and working materials needed in the department is urged by the parents. If possible, the chairman of the Parents' Committee should sit in the Primary Department conference and in other meetings where the policies and the procedures are being decided. It is very evident that to be really helpful the members of such a committee should be familiar with the curriculum and should read the current books and periodicals dealing with religious education. This does not mean that a committee less well qualified would not be helpful. A group of three or four parents who are vitally interested in the work of the Primary Department would strengthen its program.

Conferences. These will be of two kinds, occasional and regular, the latter calling for a simple organization. The occasional meetings may be at the invitation of the primary superintendent and teachers, or of the Parents' Committee. It is a good custom in some departments to have a party during the month of October, soon after the new children have come into the department from the kinder-

garten and to include the mothers in the party. Because of
the children, the party must be in the afternoon and this
means that in most instances only the mothers can attend.
If the community is such that an early evening party, say
from six to eight, could be arranged, the fathers might also
be able to attend. There may be games in which children
and mothers or parents join and then for a little while, probably twenty or thirty minutes, the parents may go to another
room where the department superintendent has a conference
with them concerning the religious education of primary children, both in the church and at home. Contacts are established which can be followed up later and the parents discover that the church school leaders are glad to receive and
to give help. When they return to the children's room, it
has been arranged for "the party," which to children is the
refreshments. The children serve their parents, the provision
always being made, of course, for a teacher or some other
friend to sit with a child whose parents cannot be there or
who has none. In addition to this combination party and
meeting there may be at least one other meeting during the
year planned especially with a program which includes opportunity for discussion and for a story hour for the children
who must attend.

Of much greater value, of course, is the regular meeting,
which can accomplish more permanent results in both home
and church. Perhaps it will be called the "Parent's Club of
the Primary Department," and it will include as honorary
members the teachers and officers of the department. Its
constitution should provide for conference between the department superintendent and the Program Committee, but
the officers should be parents. It should not be permitted to
grow into a permanent social organization or unit in the
church school, which it sometimes has a tendency to do because of the congeniality of the members. In some churches
it has been found desirable to combine the parents of children in the different departments so that those who have
children in two or more departments would not be overbur-
dened with meetings. In this case, of course, the programs
will be less specific in their nature.

Exceedingly practical problems should be discussed. Such
subjects as "Teaching Children to Pray," "Stories for Reading and Telling," "Pictures That Children Love," "The

Child's Giving to the Church School," "Race Relationship," "The Effect of the Movies on Children," are typical problems that concern both teachers and parents. Any new venture in the educational program of the church could be sponsored by such an organization. In one church which has had for a number of years a very successful expanded session, the problem was first discussed by the parents and the recommendation for the expanded session went to the Education Committee jointly from the teachers and the parents.

A circulating library which will contain not only books but magazine articles and clippings, should be provided. Government bulletins and other pamphlets on child health from the Child Study Association, Mental Hygiene Association, Iowa Child Study Association, and various insurance companies, can be made available. There should be an efficient librarian who will see that these materials are kept in circulation and that the most recent and the best books and periodicals are added to the library.

Study classes. If there is a monthly meeting for at least ten months in the year, the mothers' or parents' organization will probably find, after a year of such general discussions as have been indicated above, that they wish to enter upon a more connected study. If an hour and a half is available for the meeting, one hour of that time may be spent in the presentation and discussion of the course which they are following and thirty minutes given to problems which are common to the Primary Department and to the home.

If the class is held on Sunday morning, it should be arranged in cooperation with the Adult Department. It may be initiated by that department, in which case the primary workers will make every effort to have the parents of the children included in the membership of the class. Such a class will probably be temporary, with three or six months set aside for the special study. Helpful books and courses or units of study are available for this purpose.

SPECIFIC COOPERATION

All of these plans for meetings, organization and classes will help to create a basis for understanding and sympathy. But there are, in addition, specific matters in which the Primary Department is almost wholly dependent upon the parents for the success of its work. Either through personal contact, conferences, or study groups, this cooperation must be achieved.

Regularity of attendance. Parents who would not think of taking their children out of public school or depriving them of their Saturday music lesson, will think nothing of going away on Sunday for a considerable number of weeks during the year. If this were only during the summer season when the family is on vacation, provision could be made for these absences in the adjustment of the curriculum and the activities of the department. But a survey of the attendance of individual children will usually reveal an appalling number of absences. One mother, a member of the church, replied when the department superintendent made inquiry concerning the child, "We visit some of our relatives one or two Sundays out of every month. Of course, we can't keep the children out of school and their father is busy on Saturday, so we have to go on Sunday." In other words, the religious education offered in the Primary Department was not of sufficient importance to merit the same loyalty on the part of the family as did the work in the public school, or perhaps the requirements of the public school and the utility for material progress which would be the result of public school attendance, made it seem more important.

If the interest of the child can be so enlisted and the parents can be informed concerning the work being done in the department, and if they can be challenged by the importance of religious education in both home and school, a new attitude toward the regularity of the child's attendance will develop. Certainly the church should challenge the parents to cooperate in the matter of regular attendance. Of course, department leaders must also be very sure that the work they are doing is of sufficient value that they have a right to ask that the family shall make sacrifices in order to have the child attend regularly.

Punctuality. The attitudes which determine regularity in attendance will also affect the punctuality with which the children arrive. The department leaders should see that the parents are informed as to the time the session begins and also the time the children may arrive. If the session begins at nine-forty-five but the leaders are ready to receive the children at nine-fifteen and to provide opportunity for profitable activity, the parents should be informed of this fact. It is surprising how much more unreliable the clock at home seems to be on Sunday morning than on school mornings, but it is also true that the hour of beginning the public school is more generally known than that of the church school and leaders should make every effort to make sure that the parents know the time the child should arrive.

But an interesting program, especially something to do as soon as children arrive, will do more to bring about punctuality of attendance than anything else. When the children have nothing to do but sit or run about the building until the signal is given for an "opening exercise," there is no value and there may be even harm in their arriving early. In a good department which makes provision for the children to share in the arrangement of the room, in the planning of the work and which has many kinds of activities under way, the children will usually be insistent upon leaving home in time to join all of these interesting activities.

Teaching in the Home. There is much of religious teaching which parents will do in connection with family living. It may be unrelated to the work being done at the time in the church school but will contribute to the achievement of the same objectives. However, there are other things to be done at home which are directly related to the church school curriculum. There are stories to be read, Bible passages to be thought about and learned, poetry and songs to be enjoyed at home. Often these are suitable for use in family worship or in the child's own worship. The companionship of parents in these experiences is important. The materials are to be found in the book or leaflet which the child or his teacher brings to the home.

There will be suggestions of things to do, such as finding a picture, writing a story, making a simple investigation of some kind. These suggestions will be in the child's book or paper. Others may be included in a note from the teacher or superintendent. Still others may be given orally. If the mother will investigate all of these possibilities when the child arrives at home, and make a note of them, she will be able to assist his memory and make it possible for him to carry out his responsibility. If she thinks that what he has been asked to do is beyond his ability she should be very frank in telling the teacher or superintendent this fact. If the child has misunderstood something, or if he is apparently not interested, this should also be made known to the workers in the Primary Department. If mothers would speak directly to the teacher or leader involved the work done could be much more effective. Nearly every mother would be willing to agree to do this if it were called to her attention. Even the things that seem funny when the child has misunderstood them may be of great importance and the teacher should know about them. Friendly contact and the real spirit of cooperation will lead the mother to share this information with the child's teacher or the superintendent.

Many graded lesson courses provide a pamphlet or book for the parents so that they may see the objectives and the general scope of the work which is being attempted in the department and class. If this is not obtainable from the publisher of the lessons, the local leader should prepare some statements or make the information available through letters, articles in the church paper or information bulletins. Frequently, however, these pamphlets or books are available, but are not being used. It is essential for parents to know what the church school is doing.

The child's offering. If the parents will devise some plan, consistent with the management of their home, by which the child may do more than simply carry an offering to the church school, one phase of his religious experience may become much more valuable. Perhaps he will have an allowance, or share in giving the amount which the family budget allows for the church, or he may put it aside during the week for the special purpose of taking it to the church school. If the church provides envelopes for his use, his little box of envelopes should be among his own possessions and he should have the pleasure of putting the money into it each week. Sometimes to save trouble the mother takes care of the box of envelopes and puts the money in it and puts it in his pocket with the injunction that he be careful not to lose it and be sure that he puts it in the basket. All of which does not constitute giving on the part of the child. Talking it over at home and coming to a real appreciation of this opportunity of sharing in the work of the church, can make this a very meaningful experience for a child and one that will become increasingly so as he grows older.

These are but a few of the instances in which definite cooperation is necessary. They are also matters in which the department superintendent and teachers will probably take the initiative, although it will be very helpful to have the advice of parents who are particularly interested in the work and ready to promote it among others. During the year there will be many occasions when the success of an undertaking will depend upon the sympathetic attitude of the home. Direct contact with the home, an explanation of what is being attempted, will in nearly every instance call forth this cooperation. If the department is large and the time of the leader is very limited, the plan of sending a monthly letter into the home is most effective. These may be done on a duplicating machine, but they should be informal in their general tone. One mother had a series of more than twenty letters which she had received while her child was in the Primary Department. It is true they were form letters, but they were so personal and practical that she had saved them all and said that they had really been a course in religious education for her.

When a child feels that his mother and father and his teachers in the public school and the church school are all friends and that they love him, his world becomes a dependable, happy one, and the experiences of growing and learning bring satisfaction. When he understands that God, too, is his friend, who loves and helps him and desires his love and help in return, his world of home and church and school takes on new meanings and values.

SUGGESTIONS FOR FURTHER STUDY AND DISCUSSION

1. Plan a personal conference with the parents of a child in the department. What should be discussed? How would such a conference be followed up? What should be the outcome of such an interview?

2. Prepare a list of topics for a series of meetings of parents and teachers or a Mothers' Club.

3. Suggest several aspects of the child's religious experience in which church and home must work together.

Chapter IV

PRIMARY ROOMS AND EQUIPMENT

Preliminary Observation

1. Observe a Primary Department in session and discover what there is in the room or environment that prevents the children from (or aids them in) having experiences of worship and work.

2. Visit a good public school room for the first, second or third grade, in which the ideals of freedom and work obtain, and note the relation between the equipment and the things to be accomplished.

3. Discover children's interests in color, furnishings, equipment, as expressed in their preferences for certain places in the department or classrooms.

Six primary superintendents were asked, "If you could have what you want for your department, what would you ask for?" One of them said instantly, "More room! The children are so crowded that we can't do anything but sit!" The second said, "I'd like enough good chairs and tables." A third said, "I'd like a clean, light room. Things are so dingy that it's hard to create a happy atmosphere." The fourth said, "I'd like a place to keep my pictures and supplies." The fifth said, "My children are starved for beauty. I want the walls and furniture painted, some lovely curtains, and some good pictures." The sixth one said she didn't know but guessed they needed 'most everything.

The answers revealed not only the deficiencies of the situation in which each one worked, but something of the educational point of view of each superintendent. The first and second wanted freedom for work for their children. The third and fifth wanted beauty. The fourth wanted order but thought of the materials as hers rather than the children's. The sixth had never discovered the connection between environment and the learning process. The first five are likely to accomplish the changes they wish because they know what they want and why. The sixth will continue to have a sense of futility unless she is aroused to the point of analyzing the situation.

52

IDEALS AND IMMEDIATE IMPROVEMENT

Discovering the possibilities. There are three things which should be done by every primary leader except perhaps the one who already has ideal equipment. First, discover the greater possibilities of what is already at hand. Second, discover what changes are possible in the immediate or near future. Third, plan for the most ideal equipment, in the light of the children's needs, the local conditions, and the best educational procedure, even though the realization of this ideal seems remote.

There is scarcely any situation so hopeless that it cannot be made something nearer the ideal. A small dark basement room in a certain church seemed the most hopeless place in which a group of primary children could meet. Nothing else was available just then. But yellow paint, in three soft shades for walls, woodwork and furnishings, and ceiling, with dainty curtains at the window, made it into an entirely different place. It also proved to be a step toward the remodeling of the building and much more adequate provision for the Primary Department. Cleanliness and beauty are within the reach of any group of church leaders who are willing to work.

Frequently, there are adjustments that can be made in the church building whereby groups may exchange rooms and secure more desirable provision for the children without injury to the work of any other class or department. Additions may be built, rooms remodeled, or rooms in buildings near by may be secured and equipped. One church remodeled a small cottage at the rear of the church building facing another street so that it provided adequately for the four departments for children. It was beautiful and well equipped and worthy of its name "Children's House."

But one thing is certain, no church has ever provided ideal equipment for its children's work unless that ideal existed first in someone's mind and was the result of careful study and planning. The primary superintendent who replied, when asked how she had succeeded in securing such ideal equipment, "I had it all planned on paper for years, I prayed for it, and I worked on the building committee," had the proper combination of faith and works! Any committee on building or remodeling should include representatives of the children's departments or some provision for consultation with them.

The development of an ideal to work toward is a worthy project for a group of primary workers. What is the best approach to such an ideal? Certainly there is no one set of plans and specifications that will fit every situation. But there are certain essentials which should be included in any plan. Perhaps the questions that will discover these are: "What experiences do we hope and expect the children will have in the church as part of their growth in Christian living? What environment will make these experiences possible and most profitable?

Essentials. If we expect the children to have experiences of worship, work, appreciation, study, the environment should provide the opportunity and stimulation for them.

Space for freedom to move about; walls, floors and equipment that can be kept clean; fresh air and light; beauty that children can appreciate; protection from interruptions; substantial, comfortable furniture; good working materials and a place to keep them are all essential to a successful program of work with children. Any lack in these respects handicaps children and teachers.

Public school equipment need not be copied except in such items as are equally desirable for the church school, but the comparison between the two, which the children make, or the differences they feel, should not decrease their respect for the church. Good blackboards at school, wobbly ones at church; comfortable chairs at school, poor or broken ones at church; good pictures at school, cheap ones at church; all these make the child feel that the things he does at school are more important than the things that take place at church.

The provision for heating and ventilation should be up to the standard required for schoolrooms and a good thermometer should enable a watchful leader to regulate the temperature and secure at all times the proper amount of fresh air.

Running water should be conveniently near so that children may care for flowers, growing plants and living creatures for which they are responsible.

Location of rooms. Accessibility and sunshine are two important things to be taken into account in planning the location of primary rooms. It should not be difficult for children to reach their rooms. If they must use long dark corridors or stairways, an unpleasant connection with the church building is established. An entrance not far from an outside entrance of the building is desirable. Rooms should be on the street level or not more than one easy flight up. Sometimes the area available for educational work is limited so that there is not space for more than one or two departments on the first floor, and of course the younger children should be there. It is gratifying that the deplorable custom of putting the children's departments in the basement is disappearing.

It should also be possible for the children to get out of doors easily, especially when there is a church lawn or nearby space which may be used for certain activities. A story out of doors, or a tour of investigation and discovery, may be an important teaching procedure.

It is desirable that the rooms for the various children's departments shall be near enough to each other that intergroup activities will be possible. Doors open part of the time, friendly going in and out, sharing of interests, planned visits occasionally, all help to make an atmosphere conducive to broader experiences in Christian living.

Soundproof walls and other protections from distraction are important, but a too complete separation results in isolation and self-centeredness.

SPACE AND ARRANGEMENT

The number of rooms and their relation to each other will depend upon the plan of organization.

When the department plan of organization is used, there should be one large room and classrooms or grade rooms near by. These should be large enough to permit freedom and activity, and possible combinations of groups for special interests. Rows of doors surrounding an assembly room, leading into little classrooms in which children cannot move about freely, force the procedures into a fixed and formal pattern and neither classrooms nor assembly room serve their full purpose. When such equipment exists and cannot be changed, some way should be found either to combine some of the classrooms into larger ones, or the assembly room arranged to take care of certain kinds of activities not possible in the more restricted space of the classrooms.

Perhaps only one large department room will be available. If so, this should be arranged with the variety of activities for both the classes and department in mind. Its very appearance should suggest to the children that it is a place in which one does things and not a place for mere listening. It would be greatly to the advantage of the program if one or two additional rooms could be made available. Special groups could use these for work when necessary.

There are many two-room churches. One of the rooms is the sanctuary and used by adult and youth classes during the church school sessions. In the other, all the children's classes meet. Because they are in one room they are sometimes considered one department and are included in one assembly for worship and fellowship. Yet the differences between age groups is too great for it to be possible to meet their needs in this way. If the room is large enough, each group may have its own place for work and study and for spontaneous worship. A section of the room may be set aside as a place of worship to be used by the different age groups when they wish to do so. If a corner can be used for this purpose, the two walls, with two or three screens will make the separation complete enough to make possible the atmosphere of worship. A piano, a simple worship center, a lovely picture, and chairs not more than fourteen inches high would be the furnishings needed. The primary children would share with other children in caring for this space and at some time during the session go there for worship.

Perhaps the only space available is the corner of a one-room church. A substantial beaverboard screen for both pictures and seclusion, low chairs, small lapboards, and many other devices will help to provide the children with suitable opportunities for learning.

Space allowance. The allowance of space should be not less than fifteen square feet for each person and eighteen or twenty square feet would be better. For example, a department room for thirty children should be approximately twenty by thirty feet. It could be a little less than this if there are additional rooms available for grades, classes, or special activities. If a single grade plan of organization is used, a room twenty feet square would be desirable for a group of twenty children, a room twenty by twenty-five for a number slightly larger. Many workers feel that a rectangular room in the proportions two to three or three to four lends itself to the activities of a children's department much better than a square room, or a long narrow one.

There should be clear glass windows, placed low enough that the children can see through them. There should be enough unbroken wall space, that is without doors or windows, for the arrangement of pictures, background of scenery for plays or programs, and for the arrangement of work which the children have done and wish to share with others. The entrance to the room should be so placed that it is not likely to be at the front of groups assembled for worship, stories, or other work requiring a focus of group attention.

There should be toilet facilities adjoining the room, preferably opening into the hall or cloak room. If a cloak room is not possible, movable racks low enough for the children to reach are better than hooks on the walls, for these frequently use wall space needed for other purposes. If wall space is available, a rod with a shelf over it may be placed three feet from the floor and wraps hung on coat hangers. There should be provision for teachers' wraps and hats. A large closet or cabinet for the storing of supplies purchased in large quantities, is desirable.

Equipment. Correct posture chairs, twelve and fourteen inches high are a necessary part of the equipment. For the comfort of adult visitors a few higher chairs should be provided, but the teachers and other workers in the department will prefer chairs the same height as those used by the children.

Tables should be ten inches higher than the chairs with which they are to be used. There should be a table for each class unless the space available is limited and makes this undesirable. If having tables means that the children must sit around the tables all of the time, they should be eliminated, for they hamper the freedom of children in other activities and do not provide a good grouping for stories and discussion.

There should be tables for use in activities, for reading books, exhibits, work being done by special groups. This is the use of tables which would be provided in the separate grade room when the single grade plan of organization is followed. Small rectangular tables, about 30 by 48 or 54 inches, are desirable. They may be used for small groups or combined in various ways such as L, T, or U formation, according to the particular purpose for which the tables are used. Tables built permanently in U shape are not desirable.

There should be a cabinet or low shelves for work materials, accessible to the children. A desk for the secretary may contain such supplies as have to do with the records, teachers' quarterlies, and the other very few items which are limited to the teachers' use only. But everything which the children are to use, such as pictures, lesson leaflets or books, working materials, should be so placed that they can be responsible for them and keep them in order. When it is necessary for the equipment to be very simple, low shelves painted to match the woodwork in the room may serve the purpose and the top may be used for pictures and objects of interest. A picture file may be only a dust proof box, in which the pictures used by the classes and for the assembly are filed vertically and marked according to some appropriate classification for easy reference.

A record player and a collection of records may be used for periods of music or poetry appreciation, or for other uses when suitable records are available.

If the church has a projector for filmstrip and slides, arrangements can be made for its use in the Primary Department when needed. This will be most effective when used with a small group or class as part of a learning situation, rather than as a special feature for the whole department when it takes on the nature of entertainment. A small projector can be used on a class table without disturbing the other groups in the department. A collection of slides or filmstrip suitable for primary children and related to the units in the curriculum would be useful resource material.

There should be a good piano which is tuned at least once a year, a table for flowers, offering baskets, a good Bible with large print, and other things which may be used in periods of worship and fellowship. A low easel on which a special picture may be placed, or a poster which the children have made, will sometimes bring the picture or poster nearer to the group than when it must be placed against the wall. Blackboards to hang on the wall should be low and movable.

Arrangement of equipment. Whether it is a large department room or a single grade room, the arrangement should be as flexible as possible. Activities and experiences should not be molded to fit the equipment, but the equipment should be arranged to suit the activities. For that reason everything should be movable and substantial. Furniture should be grouped according to centers of interest, such as worship, reading, picture study, construction activities, dramatization, and other things in which the whole group or smaller groups of children will wish to engage. In fact the arrangement of the room will not merely serve the interest of children, but it will arouse new interest. The room should be a stimulating one. The superintendent and teachers may "set the stage" for activities and interests which they feel will be worth while for the children. The pictures which they find on a table or in the cabinet, a box of treasures brought back from a trip to the country, a collection of postcards from the Orient, all lead to new interest and investigation on the part of children. A place to put their work, where they can see it and where others can see it and where it can be used, stimulates the children to further achievement. While the arrangement of the equipment will be changed to suit the situation, it should be kept in mind that whenever possible the light should come from the side when the children are at work or are assembled in large or small groups.

One Primary Department of fifty children meets in a room about twenty by thirty-five feet in size. A piano, a table with flowers, a Bible, offering basket, a large framed picture of Jesus and the children, indicate that this is the center around which the children gather for worship and fellowship. There is a chair for the superintendent, but no platform, as that would separate her from the group. A long low table at one side of the room has reading and picture books for children, several collections of small mounted pictures, and a box of shells and other treasures gathered by children and teachers, indicate that this is a "browsing" table. There are chairs around the table and a few others at the side. A beaverboard screen gives a certain amount of seclusion. At another side of the room, low shelves hold work materials, and near these are several tables on which pieces of work in various phases of completion are to be seen. There are a few other tables in the room. There are enough chairs for all of the children to be seated at one time, but these are moved as the occasion requires. Some of the groups meet in an informal arrangement and others at tables, but this varies from time to time, even during the same session. The other side of the screen, which sets apart the reading corner, has on it several pictures of special interest which have been taken from the file. A group of children can gather around these and perhaps a teacher will join them, sharing their interest and appreciation and often guiding the experience.

BEAUTY AND UTILITY

Beauty in color. Mere utility is not enough in a room which is to offer the children opportunities for religious experiences. The room should have the kind of beauty which children can appreciate and enjoy. The amount of sunshine which the room has at the time of the sessions will determine to some extent the color scheme which will be used. If the room is bright and sunny, the cooler greens and blues may be used. But if the room faces north, warmer shades of yellow and buff will be desirable. The greatest care must be exercised to have artistic color combinations and to remember that Christmas and other seasons bring their special flowers and greens which must fit into the general background. Color cards are available from manufacturers of paint and enamel. These may be studied to find the most attractive combination. If for any reason it seems necessary to have the walls and the woodwork a neutral shade, color may be added in vases for flowers, soft shades in the curtains, and in good prints of pictures.

A floor covering of rubber tiling can be kept clean and decreases noise. There are also many beautiful colors to be obtained in linoleum, although the floor should not be conspicuous. If the floor covering is plain, a beautiful rug may be placed where the children gather for worship and other group interests.

Curtains should not be conspicuous in color or pattern and should serve either or both of the following purposes: to soften the bright light if the sun shines directly into the room, or to add beauty to the lines of the windows. Shades may be necessary if there is a glare of light. Even curtains may be omitted if there is not sufficient light.

A room may easily become cluttered and too full of things, even when all of them are good. If the care and beautifying of the room become an integral part of the children's activities, the changes the children make will decrease the danger of old decorations and pictures being left after their significance has passed. Artificial flowers, festoons of crepe paper, too many pictures and posters, all create confusion and hinder an appreciation of the few good things which the room should contain.

Pictures. Two or three pictures, carefully chosen, well framed and placed low, will increase the value of the room as an environment for religious growth. If the room is small and the wall space is limited there may be room for only one permanent picture. Such a one as "Jesus and the Children" by Katz, or the same subject by Clementz, may be obtained in sizes large enough for a wall picture and in good color. One of the madonnas, such as Raphael's "Madonna of the Chair," or Murillo's "Madonna With Child," is a favorite with the children. Many of the Elsie Anna Wood pictures are suitable for primary children and they are good prints and inexpensive. These and other pictures may usually be secured through denominational publishing houses.

A frame which can be opened at the back to permit the changing of pictures is a desirable piece of equipment.

There will also be the file of pictures, which are gathered from many sources and mounted on neutral cardboard, to be used in the enrichment of worship, activities, stories, and for enjoyment. Such pictures should have artistic merit in color, composition, and subject matter, and should avoid the symbolical.

The use of the room. The number of hours in which the primary rooms are used during the year is not a measure of their importance, for even if a room is in use by the children only one hour each week, it is of the greatest importance that it shall be as beautiful and useful and stimulating as it can be. But it is well for a church to consider whether or not it is getting the greatest possible value out of its investment in the equipment for the children, and this "getting the greatest value" can come only through the use of the room by the children themselves. For example, in a certain church which had made large investment in beautiful rooms, their program was expanded to include a two-hour session on Sunday, and a vacation school during the summer. This provided another sixty hours of opportunity for the Christian education of children. The room was frequently used for parties and for story hours which were held in connection with meetings to which the parents came. The policy of keeping a room tightly locked from one Sunday morning to the next is a deplorable one even when it is necessary. It would be very much better to provide supervision so that the room might be used by children at other times. In the church just described, the primary room was used one hundred and eighty-four hours during the year in which this study was made. The future will see much wider use of good educational equipment both during the week and on Sunday.

If the room must be used by other organizations during the week, it will be necessary for everything to be put away carefully after each session. There are always certain things that should be put away for the sake of cleanliness, but if the room can give an impression of use and interest, as well as of order and beauty, whenever anyone steps into it, it will be serving its purpose more fully. Someone has described a good school as "a child-size world." Children spend much of their lives in situations that are planned for adults. Even their homes must provide for grown people as well as children and the living room, dining room and many other parts of the house are full of things quite above their heads, as well as their understanding. The room to which they go when they come to the church should be planned for them, physically and spiritually. It should be a place in which they can work and which they can change and improve. It should challenge the best that they can do. It should be theirs by right of possession and not mere occupation.

Of course the most vital part of the environment is the personal element in it. This will be considered in the chapter on "Administration."

SUGGESTIONS FOR FURTHER STUDY AND DISCUSSION

1. Plan a department room, a single grade room, or a combination of department and classrooms for a department of twenty, thirty, or fifty children according to the best type of organization and the number of primary children in your church. Make the diagram on a scale of one-fourth inch for each foot of the actual dimensions and arrange the equipment according to interest centers.

2. Outline the steps in the process of changing a bare, formal room to an attractive, free, child-centered environment.

3. Plan and make a diagram of a supply cabinet and picture file, which can be used and cared for by primary children.

Chapter V

THE SESSIONS OF THE PRIMARY DEPARTMENT

PRELIMINARY OBSERVATION

Observe (or recall) a session of a Primary Department. Make a record of (a) the time given to each part of the session; (b) the way in which it began; (c) the evidences of a program having been planned; (d) ways in which it grew out of or was adjusted to the situation; (e) the extent to which the children participated in doing so; (f) the purposes or idea underlying the plans for the session and any evidences of results.

The most ideal primary rooms and equipment, the best trained teachers and leaders are all meaningless until the children enter the room. Then they become alive. Their purpose begins to be fulfilled. Theories become realities. Likewise, the point of view, the educational philosophy of the leaders stand revealed in a very short time.

One primary superintendent said at the close of a morning's session, "This has been such a good day, everything went off exactly as I planned it!" Another superintendent, in a different situation said, with equal joy and satisfaction, "This was a wonderful day, the children were full of plans and we got so many things done!"

Each of them unconsciously described her educational viewpoint as well as the session in a Primary Department.

WHAT IS A SESSION?

In the beginning it will be necessary to define what we mean by a "session." Usually we think at once of the Sunday morning session of the Primary Department of the church school, meeting in advance of or following a preaching service, or in the afternoon. Throughout this book we are thinking of a broader interpretation of the Primary Department. Any occasion when all or part of the primary children who are enrolled in the church school are together in an organization directly or indirectly under the auspices of the church, will be considered a session of the Primary Department. This may include sessions during the week, during vacation time, on Sunday afternoon or evening, and on special occasions. The procedures and experiences which are suggested or described will be quite as suitable for one of these sessions as another, the difference being found in the purposes and in the situation rather than in the time when the session occurs.

Let us recall the experiences[1] for which the Primary Department should provide opportunity: (1) joining with others in worship; (2) discussing and finding answers to religious problems; (3) working with others for worth-while ends; (4) feeling a sense of sharing in God's work; (5) being introduced to a widening world; (6) having contact with helpful adults; (7) using materials having special religious significance; (8) creating materials; (9) discovering new and helpful knowledge and skill. Considering these in relation to a session, they may be divided into four general kinds of experiences: worship, fellowship, acquiring new knowledge and learning new skills. Stated briefly, if not as accurately, they are: worship, fellowship, study and work. All of them are means of learning and growing. Permeating all of them there must be the spiritual values essential in Christian teaching: "You shall love the Lord your God with all your heart, and with all your soul, and with all your strength, and with all your mind; and your neighbor as yourself." (Luke 10:27.) These then become the elements of a session and of the program for it, and the leaders who are responsible for planning the session must discover what methods will provide these experiences.

THE MEANING OF METHOD

No discussion of primary work would proceed very far without a consideration of method, that is, if people who were actually engaged in it were discussing it. "How do you teach a new song?" "Do you believe in drill?" "How do you get the children to come on time?" Children's leaders sincerely want to do what is best, if they can discover what that is.

There are two interpretations of method, sometimes referred to as the "broad" and "narrow" meanings of the term. The "broad" meaning of method includes everything in the

---

[1]Chapter I.

total situation and considers its effect upon learning. The "narrow" meaning refers to the use of one particular way of doing a thing, but realizes that it is part of a larger situation.

For example, a group of primary children are learning a new song. Some of the children, especially the older boys, have had unsatisfactory experiences in connection with the last songs they learned and they have the feeling that they cannot sing and do not like to sing. There are also some questions in their minds about some of the things in this particular song. "How does God make all these 'things wise and wonderful'?" one child would like to ask, but has not found that a very successful way in the past of finding out things. In fact, he was reproved for interrupting the learning of a song by asking a question about it. The superintendent has just asked a question and a little girl in the group gave an answer that pleased the superintendent very much. The boy "sort of" wishes he could do something that could be approved but, on the other hand, he decides that "girls are silly" and he would rather have the other boys approve of him than the teacher. Nevertheless he has a feeling of not belonging to the group and of being "outside" the situation.

Now in the narrow sense children are learning a song, but in the broader meaning of method, there is a situation which includes the degree of friendliness existing between leader and children, the mutual respect for each other's opinion, the extent to which singing is enjoyed, and certain attitudes between boys and girls. All of these are cumulative and they change with each new situation, such as this particular instance of learning a new song.

When we consider methods in relation to the session and to elements of the program, we must remember that no method or program element is unrelated to other elements and methods, for experience is not divided into compartments. There are elements of fellowship in the exeperience of worship in a group; there is frequently an element of fellowship in work and study. A method may be chosen and used for a dominant purpose, such as acquiring knowledge, and yet its other values, such as fellowship, may be conserved. Nor are these methods and elements to be confused with periods of time in a session. Any one of them may occur at various times, either planned or spontaneously.

METHODS IN WORSHIP

Since the subject of worship will be considered more fully in a later chapter it will be only briefly described here. Perhaps "method" seems an unfortunate word to use at all in relation to worship. Yet there are different ways of worshiping and a method is a "way of doing" something. Probably the two methods of which we think at once are speaking to God in prayer and in song. Closely related to the experience of worship is the enjoyment of quiet times.

Prayer. To limit the experience of prayer to certain stated times in the session such as at the beginning, in connection with the offering, and at the close, is to fail to realize its rich possibilities. There is no part of the session into which prayer may not come as a natural and genuine experience.

Singing. Perhaps no other experience may combine more frequently and happily the experiences of worship and fellowship and learning and creativity. The very act of singing together is fellowship. Few songs may be said to embody only one of these elements. The familiar "Morning Hymn"[1] ("Father We Thank Thee for the Night") is a hymn of worship but it also includes the fellowship of living together happily. "The Many, Many Children"[2] is a song of fellowship but is worshipful in its total idea. "All Things Bright and Beautiful"[3] is a song in appreciation of nature but is also a song of worship. A group of children began to sing spontaneously, while they were at work, "There's work in the world for children to do,"[4] and their attitude expressed a sense of fellowship with each other and with God. The leader may occasionally ask herself, "Is this the best song that I can find to express that idea, and is the idea itself of sufficient importance to be included among our songs?"

The use of songs in worship will be considered more fully in a later chapter.

Quiet. Children as well as grown people need time to think, and be still. If the church could provide for children the time and place for brief moments of quiet, it would be doing them a service as great as any other that they can

---

[1] *Songs for Little People.* Pilgrim Press.
[2] *Hymns for Primary Worship.* Westminster Press.
[3] *Sing, Children Sing.* Abingdon-Cokesbury Press.
[4] Shields, *Worship and Conduct Songs.*

render. Enforced quiet becomes suppression and irritates, but the atmosphere of the session and the attitude of the leaders can help children to learn the satisfaction to be found in quiet. The children in a Primary Department were looking at a copy of Elsie Anna Wood's painting "Of Such Is the Kingdom" which is a particularly joyous portrayal of Jesus and a group of children. The leader had planned to interpret the picture and then teach Jessie Eleanor Moore's song "Long Ago the Little Children."[5] Instead she found herself singing to the children the words of the song and then keeping perfectly quiet. To have talked about the picture would have been an intrusion. For about a minute, which is a very long time for primary children to be quiet, nothing was said and each child responded to the moment according to his own thoughts.

METHODS IN FELLOWSHIP

Fellowship is a quality of feeling, not an item in a program. It is frequently a by-product of some activity but when we strive too hard to create it, it usually escapes us. All we can do is to use methods most likely to produce it.

Conversation. In every part of the session in a good Kindergarten Department, children are free to talk, to tell of their own experiences, to tell what they are thinking about the particular activity in which the group is engaged. Too often they come into a primary session in which the procedure and atmosphere are not favorable to this. One small boy had been ill at the time of promotion and had not entered the Primary Department with the group of eighteen children who came from the Kindergarten. He did not return until nearly two months later. The other children had become adjusted to the ways of the Primary Department, which was very formal and in many ways unchildlike, but he was still thinking of the church school in terms of the experiences of the Kindergarten. In the course of preparation for the offering service the superintendent asked a question which the children were to answer formally through a Bible verse; but he, out of the exuberance of his joy at being in the church school again, launched into very informal but sincere conversation in reply to her question. Almost immediately he became conscious of a disapproving atmosphere on the part of the leader

[5] *Hymns for Primary Worship*, Westminster Press.

and in the attitude of the children. He looked about him and became silent. Evidently that sort of thing was not done in this new department. Thereafter he too became a conformist and kept his thoughts to himself; but much of the joy he had found in his church was gone.

It is true that the larger number of children to be found in the departmental group sometimes makes it less easy to create the atmosphere and attitudes that are favorable to the give and take of conversation, but the leader who wants her children to be free and natural will find a way of creating conditions that are favorable to that. Of course, the natural desire of children to win the approval of the adults in any situation sometimes makes conversation very stilted and insincere. When children are saying the things that they think the superintendent and teachers would like to have them say, it is not conversation. But if a group of children work together in arranging the room, in making it beautiful, in planning a surprise for someone, then they have a great deal to say and usually considerable facility in saying it. They delight to use their growing vocabulary and a sympathetic leader can help them to express what they really think and feel.

Care and arrangement of the room. Aside from the actual cleaning of the room and the placing of such furniture as is too large for the children to manage, the care of the room may very largely be a responsibility of the children. This does not mean that every Sunday morning they will move tables and chairs and screens and arrange the room for work. But it does mean that they will frequently confer about their room and change the arrangement if it will serve their purposes better.

Play. The leader who has never played with a group of children in her department has missed the opportunity of establishing a relationship that is essential, as well as the opportunity of knowing the children much better than is possible in any situation other than play.

The vacation school, week day sessions, parties, probably offer greater opportunities for play than does the Sunday session because of its more limited time. But sometimes play will be the best method there. The children of a Primary Department were learning the song, "O'er All the World,

God's Children Play."[6] They talked about the games that children play in other lands. They decided to pretend that they were children from different countries. Five children were chosen to leave the room, each one to represent a different country. Each child knocked at the door, one of the children in the department went to the door and greeted him. He was asked to tell about the games they played in his country. Then he was asked to join the larger group. When all of the five had come in, the whole group sang "Friends,"[7] and then joined in a game on which the majority agreed. The whole thing had been quite spontaneous and grew out of one child's comment. "I wish we knew what they played," and the very evident interest of all the other children in the group. This simple form of dramatization was repeated on a number of other occasions as the children discovered new facts about their friends in other lands.

Friendly Courtesies. The celebration of a child's birthday, the coming of a new child to the department or the return of one who has been absent a long time may be occasions of genuine Christian fellowship. They should be very simple in character and genuinely religious without being unchildlike. Friends at church are glad about each other's happiness and find ways of expressing this pleasure.

METHODS IN LEARNING NEW KNOWLEDGE AND SKILLS

Discussion. The distinction between this and conversation is not always clear. According to the definitions of the two words, conversation is "an oral interchange of sentiment or observation." A discussion includes an examination into the details, a certain amount of reasoning, and a decision. The presence of a recognized problem is essential to a discussion. The leader may help to make the group conscious of the problem and may raise additional problems that help the children to think more clearly, but she should not impose her judgment upon the children nor insist that they accept her decision. Children very soon cease to enter whole-heartedly into discussions if they find that in the end they must accept the decision of an older person.

---

[6]Shields, *Worship and Conduct Songs for Beginners and Primaries.*
[7]Ibid.

There are numerous situations which may arise in a primary session in which the whole group or a portion of it may have a profitable discussion. In fact, all learning experiences involve problems and frequently a direct discussion is better than the indirect method of a story. Discussion will also grow out of stories; it will make songs more meaningful; it will lead to the discovery of beauty, as well as practical values, in the biblical material used.

Stories. Stories cannot be a substitute for the children's own thinking and decision, but they have great value in helping the children to think more clearly and to reach wiser decisions. They also have an important function in the joy which they give, for a story can frequently create an atmosphere for fuller, richer living. Perhaps a story will be an approach to worship or the interpretation of a picture or other work of art. It may give information. It may throw light upon a problem in conduct. It may come at almost any time in the session. It will, of course, be brief, and not every session will include a story.[8]

A particularly valuable use of the story, especially when the departmental plan of organization is used, is in the motivating of enterprises carried on by the whole group. For example, when a missionary project is proposed, the decision to do it and the interest in the whole enterprise will be stimulated through well-told stories about the country and the children to whom the gift is to be sent. The missionary story once a month is not as valuable as the cumulative effect of several stories, told in consecutive sessions and related to some special interest or activity. The most valuable missionary material is included in the graded lesson courses where it is an integral part of the curriculum.

The stories used by the department superintendent should usually have to do with matters of common interest to the whole group, or some need which has been discovered through observation and study, to be real in the experiences of most of the group. Care must be taken that stories told in an assembly of the entire department do not duplicate or anticipate plans which the teachers and children are carrying for-

<hr>

[8]Smither, *Teaching Primaries in the Church School*, chaps. VII and VIII.

ward in the smaller groups. In a one-hour session there is not time every Sunday for a story for the whole department nor is one necessary.

Study of pictures. This method may be introduced into the session in a very informal way or may be part of the program of worship and fellowship. There may be a corner or a panel in a screen where each week a new and lovely picture is to be seen. If one is invariably there, children will go to that place. The lighting should be good and there should be a few chairs to suggest that perhaps they would like to sit there and enjoy the picture. Usually a child will see more in a picture if an adult helps him to see certain things in it. The friendly adult who joins the group of children and talks with them about the picture will open their eyes to new appreciation.

Perhaps this picture will be talked about later as part of the fellowship or in preparation for worship or for the planning of some work. However, it is not necessary that the picture shall always be talked about. It may be there just to enjoy.

Sometimes the picture is there for sheer beauty, such as a lovely autumn scene or spring picture. Pictures are valuable resource material to which children may turn for information they need in carrying on activities. When there is a file which children can reach and from which they may select pictures, there will be an additional interest in and appreciation of the pictures which are used in the department room.

Appreciation of poetry. The leader who seats herself with a group of children gathered about her, informally if possible, and reads to them some poems which she honestly enjoys, finds that the imagery and rhythm of poetry open doors which children gladly enter. Sometimes a poem is about some daily experience, or about something the children love, or something they love to do. The poem, "A Wish Is Quite a Tiny Thing," from *Silver Pennies,*[9] would lead to some very interesting ideas in any group of children. In the same book, "The Little Jesus Came to Town," is a lovely thing. Perhaps the children will be introduced to a song first as a poem and learn to love it, then be delighted when they discover that there is music for it. Or, perhaps they will like a poem so well that

---

[9]Thompson, *Silver Pennies.*

they compose music for it themselves as one group of children who said, "That poem just ought to be a song. Let's make it into one!"

Nearly all children make up rhymes and when they hear over and over again lovely poems, they find a joyful release of spirit in the making of poems that say the things they feel.

Books of poetry for children should be included on the reading table and frequently a child will discover something that meets the need of his own spirit. Perhaps he cannot read all of it and will be happy when a teacher or leader sits down beside him and helps him to read it or reads it to him.

Appreciation of music. When children hear music they usually respond to it in some way other than just listening. Sometimes this response is a physical one according to the rhythm of the music. Or they make up words to it and sing them, or they tell of what it reminds them. Sometimes this response will be superficial, but that will be because children are not skillful in expressing their deepest feeling. The learning and growth which may come through listening to music justify the use of this method.[10]

If a good pianist is not available, beautiful music may be brought to the children through the Victrola or a similar instrument. They may be purchased for a very small amount. Even the small portable ones are very effective. A list of fine records will be found in the book just referred to.

Reading. The newly acquired skill of reading is a joy to nearly all primary children except a few to whom the process is a painful one. The library or browsing table has been referred to several times. It is not an uncommon thing for primary children to come early to the church in order to spend some time at the reading table.

The reading ability of children of primary age varies in different communities according to the methods of the public school. The leaders of the Primary Department in the church can discover the type of books which are used in the first three grades of the public school and be governed by this in their selection of books for the reading table in the department. If the public school does not provide a rich supply of reading

[10]See Chapter VIII in Music in the *Religious Growth of Children*, by Elizabeth McE. Shields.

books for children, perhaps the church can supplement this with general books on poetry, art and stories. But usually the church can limit its reading books to those which are either specifically religious in their nature or most likely to lead into experiences of world friendship, good will and friendly cooperation. Nature study books, suitable for children this age, frequently lead to new appreciation of God's world and our share in making it beautiful. Books in all of these fields should be placed on the reading table when they are appropriate to the unit being used with the children.

Reading to the children. There is also a place for reading aloud. Children enjoy hearing an adult read selected passages from the Bible, when it enriches an ongoing experience and when it is read well. Certain psalms and even familiar stories take on new beauty when they are read to the children by an appreciative leader. One primary superintendent frequently sat down with the children of her department and read to them a lovely passage from the Bible. One boy went home and said, "Mother, I certainly will be glad when I am old enough to read the Bible myself. If I had one now I think I'd ask Miss Brown to mark the places she reads to us, so that I would be sure to find them when I was big enough to read them."

Memorization. By memorization is meant the repeated use of a song, poem, or passage of Scripture, until the words have been learned. A judicious use of this procedure will result in the children's knowing certain things which they will enjoy and use. Before learning any portion of a song, poem or Scripture passage, the children should have heard all of it and discovered its meanings. It is not conceivable that we would take the time to have children memorize anything that we did not want them to use and love as a cherished possession. Yet sometimes the dullness and weariness of drill spoils material which otherwise the child would enjoy.

A group of primary children who were learning the Christmas story as it is found in Luke 2:8-12, disliked it thoroughly by the time they had memorized it. If they had first learned to love it as a series of word pictures, and to associate with it other pictures and songs, the desire to learn it would have carried them through the process of memorization.

There are no mechanical formulas to be memorized as an introduction to Christian living. The spirit is always more important than the letter. The child who has learned to look upon Jesus as a great leader, to love hearing the things he said when he was on earth and who really wants to live as he lived, has a far better preparation for Christian living than one who can repeat the Beatitudes. They are largely outside the experience of primary children, but will become meaningful and beautiful when experience interprets them later. Our joy in them at the right time may even be marred by an insistence upon learning them before the mind and heart have been made ready through experience. Therefore, we will help children to acquire the things they can love and appreciate now, that they would like to have as their own, even as they may own a picture. Frequent use of Bible passages, songs, poems, and their association with each other, with pictures, with worth-while experiences, will help children really to "learn" them and not just to know the words.

In learning songs it is usually best to learn the music and the words together, hearing the song sung first and then learning parts of it by singing them. Otherwise a great length of time for drill is required if the two processes are carried on separately. Songs will, of course, be selected that are within the voice range as well as the vocabulary and experience of primary children. Most authorities agree that the range of the primary child's voice is from E to upper F. High, light tones are easiest and best.

Perhaps we would feel that to be consistent with our educational theory that we should begin with the interest of the children, we should let them choose the songs which we are to use and be guided by their choice. Certainly the children may have a share in choosing the songs that are to be learned, but the songs from which they make their selections should be good, so that any choice would be a suitable one. A group of children will enjoy gathering around a piano, before the session some morning, and helping the leader or the pianist to choose a new offering song, after they have heard two or three played and sung. But no song that was not worthy should be included in those from which they choose.

LEARNING THROUGH CREATIVE WORK

The deepest feelings do not come to primary children through seeing what others have done, even though it may be beautiful and wonderful. Their truest appreciation of pictures will come when they themselves create. One group of second-grade children in the Primary Department painted a series of pictures of the lovely things they had seen on a little trip to a woods near town, looking for wild flowers. The Sunday after their trip they painted the pictures and then arranged them and announced to the rest of the department that they were holding an art exhibit on the screens around the place where their group met. They announced that the subject of their art exhibit was "The Wonders in God's World." They explained that they had not picked any of the wild flowers because they wanted to leave them for other people to enjoy, but they had made pictures of some of the most interesting and beautiful things they saw. The other grades visited their exhibit that morning. Large sheets of white drawing paper, bottles of tempera paints (made from powder paint), some brushes not too small, provided the working materials from which the children selected what they needed for carrying out their purposes.

Construction work. This type of work will probably arise most frequently in connection with the work of grades or small groups. However, there are times when the children will wish to make certain things in connection with projects they are planning and carrying on as a department. One group of children made a series of peep boxes, during the work period, all of the group sharing in it and resulting in a "Journey to Many Lands" exhibit to which parents and other friends were invited. An experience of working together in this way offers an opportunity for cooperation between older and younger children and for a wider range of personal contact than a child may find in only one class group. Freedom to choose and plan, simple working materials, assistance when needed, are all essential if construction work is to have educational value. It will be much more fruitful in Christian living if it is an undertaking carried on in cooperation with others.

There is always the possibility that in an intensely interesting session children may be overstimulated. Sometimes it is good for a child to be let alone, provided he does not want to be alone too much and does not have a tendency to morbidness. The writer remembers one energetic little girl who worked hard in whatever enterprise happened to be under way and who was a very social little person. One day she left the group at work and walked with great determination over to a table at the other side of the room. The leader noted it and by and by went over to her. Before she could ask a question, the little girl looked up at her with an expression that dared anyone to interfere with her. Emphatically she said, "I'm going to look at these books. I've wanted to so long!" And then the leader realized that while no activities had been forced upon any of the children, the momentum of the situation had carried them on until they really had very little choice in the matter.

In nearly every session there may be opportunity when individual children, having completed some particular thing for which they are responsible, may have some free time to follow out individual interests. When children can withdraw from the group occasionally there is less danger of nervous strain and overstimulation.

Always we must remember that the session is for children, not a fixed program to which children must conform rigidly.

SUGGESTIONS FOR FURTHER STUDY AND DISCUSSION

1. From your own memory or an interview with a primary superintendent, make a list of the methods used in a Primary Department session over a period of four or five weeks, to discover the variety and worth of what was done.

2. If the children in your Primary Department were not responsive or original, how would you go about changing the condition?

3. Make a list of the songs used in the course of a year or eighteen months in a Primary Department with which you are familiar, and classify these according to their purpose and content.

4. If possible, secure the cooperation of the pianist and have an informal period with a group of children who come early, gathered around the piano, discussing and choosing a

song to be used in the session. Note what the children say
and what is evidently the basis for their choice. Note their
attitude toward the song when it is introduced to the whole
department later.

5. Discuss with some child or group of children the things
that they do in the Primary Department at church and discover what they like, and what they do not like, and why.

Chapter VI

PLANNING THE SESSION

Preliminary Observation

1. Experiment with one or two of the methods described in the preceding chapter and note the way in which you found it necessary to adjust your procedure to the children's interest.

2. Make a list of the methods used in the Primary Department you observed last week and make note of others that you think might have been used to better advantage.

3. Observe a primary grade in a good public school and note what opportunities there were for pupil initiative and for ways in which the teacher followed the lead of the children's interests.

——————————

The wise leader will sit down as soon as possible after one session of the department and begin to think about the next one. While the experiences of the day are fresh in her mind, she will make notes concerning needs that were revealed and that could not immediately be met, conduct problems that were evident, things the children said about what they would like to do, or something they would like to find out, the general atmosphere of the department. For example, perhaps certain children in the group are dominating the situation to such an extent that other less aggressive children are not having an opportunity for their share in the planning and activity of the department. Or, perhaps interest in some undertaking has become so intense that the purpose of getting it done satisfactorily has caused some unhappiness and the good will and joyousness of fellowship have suffered. Perhaps some child who is a bit of a bungler but nevertheless loves to help, has been made very unhappy. In other words, good will is being sacrificed for thoroughness. The leader faces the problem, in planning the next session, of choosing activities and program materials that will supply these interests, meet these needs, correct the undesirable attitudes.

Seasonal interests. There are seasonal experiences of the children to be taken into account, interests which loom large in the children's lives, or others which are important and might be overlooked. A wise leader will make note of these interests and make them an avenue of enriching the religious experiences of the child.

Group activities. There are activities which are going on in the smaller groups. In the department plan of organization these are class groups. In the single grade or department unit plan, they are interest groups. It is not necessary to coordinate all of these with department activities, nor to coordinate the program of the department with all of the group activities, but there are certain of them which involve intergroup activities or which are more effective when they can be shared with the other children of the department. There is a need for the interweaving of interest and activities between the groups.

Emergencies. There are also emergency situations which must be taken into account. Perhaps these can scarcely be considered as part of a plan made in advance, because frequently they occur too late to be planned for. But when there has been a community disaster during the week or radio and headlines tell of war or other disasters, it is reasonably certain that the primary children will be excited about it and also frequently true that they will have overheard adult conversations which give a religious implication to the event. The wise leader will plan a session or a series of sessions that will help the children think more clearly about how God works in the world, what he expects of us at such times, and to feel secure in his love, even though neither they nor the adults in their world can always feel physically safe.

The children's interests. The children themselves will have a large share in determining the direction the session will take, if their initiative has been encouraged and allowed to find expression in the activities of the group. For example, a department superintendent who had planned to tell a story might find herself involved instead in a discussion, launched by the children and growing out of some activity. She would be very unwise indeed, if the discussion is a profitable one, to insist upon interrupting it in order to tell the story she had planned. Perhaps she had brought a picture which she had expected would serve as an approach to a new song, but instead she found the interest in the picture itself so great that an interpretation of that seemed the most desirable thing and the most fruitful, so that a picture appreciation took the place of learning a new song for that particular session.

All of this makes it necessary to face the problem of how any plan can be made for a session in advance. Yet the leader who has no plan is at a serious disadvantage and usually gives evidence of it in the uncertainty of her leadership. No matter how good her educational background may be, how sound her educational theory, or how rich her resources, it is necessary to make certain plans if her leadership is to be effective.

The plan. But of what will the leader's plan consist? Would it be a program of songs, prayer, picture verses, stories, and other materials? Certainly these would be included and the plan would also contain alternative materials. If the leader profits by past experience and cultivates her imagination a little, and if she knows her group of children, she will be able to have some general idea of what will probably occur, although she may not know the exact trend that it will take. Perhaps the thing she plans to do one Sunday will fit another occasion even if it had to be abandoned on the day for which she planned it. She will also be very wise if she makes notes on her plans, after the session, indicating how the plan was modified or changed, and why.

SEQUENCE IN A SESSION

A primary leader who is sensitive to the interests of children and the factors mentioned above, will probably not know the exact sequence in which the program will develop. When the department is organized on the single grade or departmental plan the experiences of the session may follow the needs and interests of the children. Even then the work of different interest groups must be considered. When different grades and classes are using the same room, or are joining in the same assembly for worship and fellowship, there must be a certain schedule so that the teachers, as well as the departmental leader, can be ready to guide the work in the group for which they are responsible. But it is doubtful if it is necessary, even then, to have a rigid time schedule. Certainly the plan of having children assemble on the click of the clock for fifteen minutes of worship, followed by a fellowship period of ten minutes, a march to classes at a certain time, and a return for dismissal, does not permit a very natural or spontaneous religious experience on the part of the children. Custom and the limitations of rooms and equipment may seem to make such a rigid program necessary, but it is usually possible to secure greater flexibility when there is a desire on the part of leaders and teachers to provide the children with the best opportunity for work and worship.

For example, in one department which was organized on the department basis, with smaller class groups, and which had only the limited one-hour schedule, all too meager at best, the leader made out a tentative schedule for each morning. A copy of this she placed on a bulletin board above the secretary's desk. The teachers read it as they came in. Perhaps it would read something like this, "Work (interest or class groups) 9:15 to 9:45." (The formal time of opening the school was 9:30. Thus work began fifteen minutes before the regular time of opening the session and extended beyond that time fifteen minutes.) Under the heading of this period were listed the various activities that would probably be going on. Some of these were class groups who had work under way. Other children would be arranging and caring for the room and there was a group project in which the entire department was interested. The library table was also listed as one of the activities. Thus there were five kinds of probable activities listed under the first heading.

The next item on the tentative schedule was, "9:45 to 10:00, Worship and Fellowship." Under this were listed some of the materials (songs, Scripture, story and other things) that would probably be used and the particular problem around which the period had been planned by the leader and which had grown out of something that had taken place the week before. Perhaps it would seem that this fifteen minutes is entirely too brief a period for worship and fellowship, but it must be remembered that there would certainly be fellowship and sometimes worship connected with the work of the smaller groups. The next item on the tentative program was "10:00 to 10:30, Class Groups." The groups did not reassemble for dismissal, but each teacher planned for this in her own class.

It was quite definitely understood by the superintendent and the teachers that perhaps this sequence would not be followed. Especially if a number of the class groups were engaged in activities in the work period, it might be very much better to have the class groups immediately follow the work period and have the worship and fellowship at the close. Or perhaps the time for work at the beginning would be shorter, depending upon what there was to be done. There might be a brief period of fellowship which emerged from the work period and took place wherever the activities were being carried on, without taking the time to assemble and thereby losing the timeliness of the situation. After this, the children might go to their class groups and return for a period of worship at the close.

Changes in the plan or schedule will be made on the basis of the leader's observation of what is going on in the smaller groups, upon suggestions and requests which come from teachers and children, and upon evidences of needs or interests. She will make sure that it does not seriously affect the work of any group. If a change is to be made, the leader will quietly let the teachers and leaders of the smaller groups know what change is being made. This can be done without interrupting the work of any group, even when they are meeting in separate rooms. Quietness and ease of manner, as well as alertness, are essential for the leader of an informal session.

If the department had been organized on the single grade plan or the department unit, the leader would have maintained similar relations with the assistant teachers. Even though the initiative would have rested to a greater extent with the leader and the program would have been even more flexible, it is still important that the assistants shall know what materials and procedures will probably be used.

Slavishly following a pattern for a session, administered according to a bell which is rung in some central place in the church building, is unnecessary in nearly every instance. Flexibility can be secured when the leaders desire it.

AVAILABLE TIME

"Where can I find the time to do all of these interesting things?" is the despairing question in the minds of hosts of children's leaders who are discovering the possibilities of religious education. It takes time for children to make plans and to carry them out. The initiative and originality of children do not emerge under the pressure of hurry. When the time is short the leader must be very sure that the most essential things are provided for. Too often the leader will feel that the most essential things are the things that she herself does and will feel that there is no time for the children to discuss, make plans, work together and engage in actual experiences of Christian living. "We still think that children can learn by being told things!" The less time there is, the more sure must the leader be that the greatest possible opportunity is given to the children for their own creativity and that the minimum of time is used for the part which she herself does.

Before the scheduled time of beginning. This time has frequently been called the pre-session period. But in reality it is part of the session. There are nearly always children who arrive ten or fifteen minutes before the time announced for the beginning of the school. This will vary in different communities. If the work is interesting enough, the children will find a way to be there.

One morning, in a certain Primary Department, there were twenty-five children out of the forty usually in attendance, who were busily engaged in all sorts of activities when the general superintendent of the school put his head in the door ten minutes before the appointed time of beginning. "When does this department start?" he asked the secretary. "I don't know," she said; "they were busy when I got here ten minutes ago." The primary superintendent overheard the conversation and said, "Well, it began this morning at nine o'clock, when Billy and I got here and went to work." And, of course, that is when any session begins, when someone comes and begins to work.

Lengthening the session. When only an hour or even less has been provided for the session of the Primary Department, it is frequently possible to secure an extension of this to one hour and a quarter. A church which had been having a school session of only one hour, the preaching service of an hour and a half, found that it was possible to readjust their program so that the school session might be extended fifteen minutes. It is surprising how much of the pressure of haste may be removed and how many more things may be done when even this brief additional time of fifteen minutes becomes available. Certainly no session of a Primary Department should be less than one hour and a quarter in length.

The expanded session. There are an increasing number of churches who are finding it possible and advisable to expand the sessions of their children's department to two hours or two hours and a half in length, thus extending through the period of the adult church service. Local conditions, the distances people must travel to get to the church and home again, the suitability of the building for such a program, must all be taken into account. The leaders will also wish to be sure that they are prepared to guide the children into fruitful religious experiences for this longer period of time.

When the education committee and the children's leaders feel that they are ready to attempt this expanded session, it will be necessary to create public sentiment and to counteract the effect of the many years in which people have thought of the church school in much more limited terms than we are thinking of it today. Sometimes parents who think that children sit still and listen for the greater part of the session feel that a period of two hours would be entirely too long. When they understand the teaching procedures which are used and the greater freedom and activity which the children have, this objection will no longer be felt.

Sometimes there is the feeling that children, with their parents if possible, should be in the preaching service. Leaving aside the question as to whether or not this could be achieved in the Protestant church of today, one must face the question squarely as to whether or not it is desirable. If it can be spiritually profitable for children to attend habitually a service which they cannot understand, and if this is better than anything else that might be provided for them, then the educational forces of the church should bend their efforts in that direction. But if it is important that the child shall understand what he does and shall be an active participant, then the church should provide him the largest possible opportunity for those experiences. Perhaps it will be said that there are things that the child may feel but cannot understand and that the experience of being in a beautiful church sanctuary, hearing the music and feeling the atmosphere of worship, are valuable experiences in themselves. It is equally true that the sense of repression, of being outside what is really going on, and of trying in vain to understand, are unprofitable, and may even be harmful experiences.

If there is an expanded session of the Primary Department, extending through the time of the church service, provision may be made occasionally for the children to go into the sanctuary and join with the others in a portion of the worship service. They should be prepared for such an experience by having explained to them in advance what will happen while they are there. If the children have previously visited the sanctuary and have had opportunity to explore it, they will feel less strange when they go to it at the time of a church service.

When the expanded session is two hours or more in length, it is sometimes difficult to preserve unity throughout the session. There is danger that even the leaders will talk about the "first hour," and the "second hour." This is especially true when there is a change in leadership. When the primary work is organized on the departmental basis with small classes, it will probably not be necessary for the entire staff to remain through the entire session.

One expanded session was planned on a schedule something like this: At ten o'clock there was time for fellowship. The children were not encouraged to arrive until ten o'clock. The few who came in advance of that time arranged the room and engaged in activities in class groups or interest groups. All or most of these activities had been planned the week before and were part of the ongoing units of work. Sometimes the children gathered informally to make and discuss reports growing out of work that had been done. New plans were proposed and discussed, or arrangements made for a later discussion of them. Other experiences of fellowship such as the greeting of new pupils and visitors and children who had returned after an absence, took place informally. At about ten-twenty the groups began their work. Some of these groups were in separate rooms and others met in portions of the assembly room. The children were not crowded and there was freedom to move about, to go to other parts of the room and to vary the activities, as the class periods were about forty minutes in length. Since the procedures could be varied the children were not tired at the expiration of the time.

At about eleven o'clock they gathered in the portion of the room that was arranged for worship and a period of preparation and worship followed. Sometimes they went out of doors for a walk or in summer weather they gathered in a circle on the lawn. Once they went to the home of a former teacher in the department who had been ill and who lived not too far away. They had a genuine experience of worship and fellowship there.

In this particular department there were twelve people on the staff, eight of them teachers. Sometimes at the beginning of this period, or sometimes at the close, some of them (usually four or five) slipped away from the group, the children understanding of course that they had gone to the church sanctuary to join in the worship there. A schedule was arranged by the teachers so that they could take turns remaining throughout the department session. This was done on the basis of units rather than weeks.

At about eleven-twenty there was an informal period when projects, discussion groups, reading groups, the library table, the planning and doing, all found their place. These were not unrelated activities. All of them were part of the program of work in the department. Sometimes there was a story, or a book was read aloud, when either of these seemed desirable procedures in connection with the work that was going on. A few moments before twelve o'clock the materials were put away, the children who were responsible for certain duties about the room performed them, and the children were ready to join their parents or older brothers and sisters at twelve o'clock.

In the beginning the leaders had felt that a period of play should precede the work, but the children soon became so interested that one of them seemed to express the mind of all of them when she said one day, "Do we have to stop and play? Can't we begin our work right away?" After that, play found its natural place in the session and sometimes grew out of the story or the plans which the children made. That is, if play seemed to be a good thing to do in that particular connection, they played; but it was not found necessary for sake of physical activity, since the other procedures used offered sufficient freedom of movement. There are almost an unlimited number of ways in which the schedule for an expanded session may be worked out. The one that has been described is only one of them.

The Junior Congregation. Sometimes the primary children are included in a Junior Congregation. Such an arrangement is undesirable because the program will be too old for them (or if not, too young for the juniors), they will be asked to engage in a session which is not suited to their needs, and the leadership they have in the church on Sunday will be divided so that there will be danger of duplication, as well as of serious omission in the experiences. For example, they will have a worship service in the Primary Department, and another in the Junior Congregation. They will hear and learn certain biblical material in the Primary Department and again in the Junior Congregation. Probably service activities will be set going in both places and the child finds himself with a divided loyalty without knowing why or being able to defend himself against it. An expanded session for each department (primary and junior) will offer a better opportunity for unity of purpose and program.

Children's organizations. A number of denominations are finding it possible to make the curriculum and organization of the various age groups so inclusive and complete that separate organizations for special interests are not necessary. All the children share in all the activities and interests of the church's program.

If for any reason there must be any other organization for children it should be graded so that it is not necessary for primary and junior children to be included in the same organization. The program materials and the activities of such an organization should be considered part of the curriculum of the Primary Department. They should be selected with as much care as anything which enters into the experiences of the children.

The Church School of Missions. The sessions of this school usually meet in the evening for a period of six or eight weeks during the winter. Its sessions are early in the evening and frequently groups for children are provided. So with primary children the material used should be selected with the whole curriculum in mind.

Sessions during the week. Sometimes the limitations of the church building and other conditions make it impossible to have an expanded session on Sunday, and provision can be made for the whole department or groups within it, to meet during the week, coming to the church after school, or on Saturday morning. The leadership should either be the same as on Sunday or there should be provision for the conferences necessary to work out a program in which there is unity of purpose and sufficient diversity of material and procedure. This weekday session will probably be of the nature described in the work period of the expanded session, with the addition of a certain amount of more formal instruction, that is, stories, the learning of new songs, and of Scripture material, but all of these should be related to the work of the session and as far as possible the weekday and Sunday sessions should be integrated. That is, there will be carry-overs, such as reports on Sunday of plans that the children made and have been working on during the week. The weekday and Sunday sessions will make use to some extent of the same songs and have other materials in common. They are in reality, two sessions of the same school.

The community weekday school. When the weekday religious education is organized on a community basis, there are certain adjustments which must be made if the children's experience is to have unity and the two organizations are to avoid working at cross-purposes. The fact that the children are under different leadership, with a different group of children and meeting under entirely different conditions, complicates the problem but does not make it impossible of solution. Such community weekday schools usually have a plan by which all the different churches share in the administration of the weekday school. Each church is represented by one or more persons on the Board of Administration. It is even more important that the Education Committee of the church and especially the department leaders, shall share in the work of setting up objectives, selecting materials and activities.

It is probably not possible to correlate closely the work done in the Sunday sessions and in the weekday schools under conditions such as these, but it is possible to work together for common purposes and for each to enrich the work of the other.

The vacation church school. Whether the church conducts its own vacation school or cooperates with other churches in the community, the work done in the vacation school should be looked upon as an integral part of the program for primary education in the church. The same opportunities for consultation and for conference in the setting up of objectives and programs should be provided. Cooperation in the use of equipment and work materials should be made possible. It is most unfortunate if children feel that their leaders on Sunday are not pleased when the room and the materials have been used by the vacation school leaders. Children very quickly sense an attitude of this kind. They should be conscious of the fullest sympathy on the part of all of the leaders of the church and should feel that the vacation school is just another session of their Primary Department. Perhaps there will be other children who are not members of their Sunday session who will be in the vacation school, but this will be an opportunity for an enlarged fellowship and for sharing their room and materials with other children. When a church has a vacation session there are certain activities which might otherwise be included in the Sunday morning session which can be omitted and left to the vacation school to carry out.

When local conditions make it possible to have the same teachers in both vacation and Sunday morning sessions, or at least some of the same teachers, the opportunity to integrate the program is greatly increased. Some denominations are building a year-round program of religious education with the Sunday, vacation, and weekday sessions all integral parts of it.

Basis for cooperation. When there are various sessions of the Primary Department, under different leadership, these leaders must face together the questions: What are the needs of our children? How may these needs be met? What procedure shall we use? What differences, if any, shall there be between the different sessions? What materials and plans shall be the special resources and responsibility of each session? How can we help the children to feel that there is unity of leadership and work in all of their church school experiences?

SUGGESTIONS FOR FURTHER STUDY AND DISCUSSION

1. Plan a session for one hour, one hour and a quarter, or two hours, according to your own situation. Indicate the probable interests of the children, their needs, the procedures you would plan to use and the way in which the exact order of the session and the choice of materials could be adjusted to meet the situation.

2. If you became superintendent of a Primary Department which had been very formal and in which the children apparently lacked interest and originality, how would you proceed to change the situation?

3. What would be the basis for deciding when an expanded Sunday morning session was desirable and what would be the best steps to take in preparing for it?

Chapter VII

THE WORSHIP EXPERIENCES OF PRIMARY CHILDREN

PRELIMINARY OBSERVATION

1. Recall or enter into some experience with children in a worship service planned for or by them. Did you feel worshipful? Was there evidence that the children really worshiped? If so, what contributed to the experience? If not, what hindered it?

2. Recall from your own experience and from the observed experience of children, evidences that worship has produced changes in attitude, work, and play.

We know so little of what really goes on in the minds of children, their thoughts, their emotions, their motives. Least of all can we feel sure that we are able to understand in any measure the worship experiences of children. Surely we will not expect them to be like those of a mature Christian, although maturity in the Christian life is not always a matter of years. Perhaps a child looks upon God as a magician who makes things happen and can, if he wishes, do what we want him to do. Or perhaps, this magic working God can give us anything that we want, and so the child's prayers are largely those of petitions for the dog he wants so much, or a pony, or a baby brother. Or he may seem to the child to be a righteous God whose disapproval is to be greatly feared, and so the child's prayers are in the nature of propitiation.

Fortunate indeed is the child whose experiences have brought him to these years of middle childhood with a firm belief in God's infinite love and goodness and the realization that God desires above all else the love of his children for each other and for him. Such a child fears to do wrong not because of dread of punishment, but because it would be failing to do what one whom he loves expects him to do. The little boy who said, "You see God is counting on me to do that and I just can't let him down," had the spirit that underlies worship and all Christian living. His faith is not dependent upon this getting what he wants when he asks

God for it, or escaping punishment when he knows that he has done wrong. His faith transcends all of these things because it is an all pervading sense of love received and given.

The child in whose world the grown people are dependable and loving and understanding, of course, has much less difficulty in attaining this interpretation of God. But the child who lacks those things in his human relationship may be helped through sympathetic and affectionate guidance to find in the experiences of worship and work in the church school, that stability which comes only through confidence in a God who loves and cares.

It is one of the functions of administration to provide the environment and opportunity for worship, and it is that function with which we are concerning ourselves in this chapter. Through the administration of the department, the leader and her associates will answer such questions as: What environment is most conducive to worship? What hymns, poems, Scripture material, pictures, activities, will help children to discover their own need of worship and to find satisfaction in the experience?

WHEN WILL WORSHIP OCCUR?

Planned occasions. There will be occasions when definite provision is made for worship. That is, the leader in planning a session, or a series of sessions for a Primary Department or grade group, will plan the time and place and procedure for worship, although all of these may be, and probably will be, adjusted to meet the situation as it develops.

The plans for worship at these times will take into account the religious problems of children such as: What God is like, how he works in the world, how we work with him, how he cares for us, the meaning of prayer, all in the terms of a child's feeling and thought rather than adult theology. Sometimes these problems will be revealed to the leader by things the children say or do. They may be suggested by the teachers or assistants. But they may also come from the leader's knowledge of child life. Certainly we will not wait for children as a group or as individuals to raise great religious problems before we mention them. The risk would be too great. Children may be prepared to meet problems with right thinking and to grow spiritually by doing so.

Frequently those planned occasions will grow out of the experiences the children are having in their class or interest groups, and should always be related to them. The children may bring to the larger group discoveries they have made, problems they want to talk about (which will lead to worship) and things they wish to share, a hymn they have written or learned, a poem, a prayer, a picture. These will often be part of the course of study. In turn the teacher or leader of the smaller group will use the experiences of worship and fellowship in the larger group for the further development of the work in her group.

If a grade or group has a complete session in a separate room and the group is not large the time for worship will occur whenever the situation is most suitable.

In relation to activities. Worship may take place in connection with an informal group activity. Sometimes the joyousness of an experience out of doors or of looking at a lovely picture or of hearing a story about someone who has done something fine or great, or hearing of the needs of children elsewhere, will lead children to desire to talk to God about it. Just as it is natural for children to be eager to tell mother or father about anything, good or bad, that has happened or about which they have heard, so is it natural for children to whom God is a real friend and loving Father, to want to tell him about the things they enjoy or the things that are hard for them.

A group of children were at work on some gifts they were sending to a home for crippled children. They had chosen the particular things they were making and had entered upon the work with great enthusiasm. But it proved to be a little more difficult than they had anticipated and to call for a great deal of patience and perseverance. There was a sense of failure developing in the group and a little irritability. As the end of the work period was drawing near one Sunday, the leader voiced the feeling that the children evidently had and said, "Is this too hard for us? Do you think we had better give it up?" The children were very unhappy at the thought and they all sat down together and analyzed their difficulty. They discovered the things that were too hard for them to do and decided to ask a boy in the Intermediate Department to come in and help them the next week.

They also found the places in which they were not being careful enough. Then plans for going ahead with the under-taking were made.

The leader could feel that the children were not entirely satisfied, that there was something lacking and so she said quite naturally and simply, "Shall we talk to God about it?" Most of the children nodded and only a few looked the least bit self-conscious. One very practical boy said, "Well, he is counting on us to do this and we'd better tell him how it is." So the leader led in a very simple prayer, "God, our Father, we came to a hard place in our work. Some of it we were not doing very well and we are sorry. Some of it is too hard for us and we are going to ask someone to help us. Help us to do the very best we can and to make the crippled children happy. We are glad that we have straight legs and strong arms. Amen." The joyousness of the children after the discussion and prayer made it evident that both had been necessary. Prayer as a means of discipline would be unthink-able. But prayer as a means of getting new courage and determination is a vitalizing Christian experience.

Sometimes the sense of companionship with God does not become so articulate. A group of children were having a happy experience working together and one of them said, "I'll bet He's glad we are having such a good time." Every-one seemed to know who the child had meant and they all joined quite spontaneously in the song, "There's work in the world for children to do." They had been aware of fellow-ship with God and felt sure he knew they were happy.

In the small group. Worship will also enter into the experi-ences of a class or interest group. Even if a group does not have a separate room or any seclusion, it is still possible for the children to have moments of worship together when these come as the result of a real need or desire felt by the children. There may be certain times, more than others, according to the lesson materials or activities that are being carried on in the group, when worship will be a natural part of what they are doing.

Personal worship. Of course the child will have worship experiences when he is alone and when he is at home. Some of these will be at appointed times, such as his prayer at night or in the morning, the grace at the table, and other times when the family worships together. It is to be regretted that these occasions are not more frequent and that when they do occur they are not more childlike and natural. The child's experiences in the church school will help to make these times of worship outside the school more meaningful. They should help him to discover occasions and ways of speaking to God. They will help to make worship seem natural and real, as well as satisfying. Church school workers can be helpful by suggesting books of devotional material for use with children at home.[1]

WHAT FORMS AND MATERIALS WILL CHILDREN USE IN WORSHIP?

The child's spontaneous expression. Another form of the question above may be: To what extent shall children use forms and materials in worship? Certainly not to the exclusion of their own spontaneous expressions. To substitute even a really good prayer-poem for something a group of children want to say to God, their Father and Friend, would hinder worship rather than enrich the experience.

The function of any worship material should be threefold and enable the worshiper to say what he feels but is unable to express adequately; to enrich and give deeper meaning to his ideas and feelings; to lead to greater freedom in spontaneous expression. These three functions may be applied as tests in the selection of worship material.

One answer to the original question is that they will use the forms and materials to which they are introduced, and this places upon the leaders in the church school the responsibility of making available to children materials which they can use and of guiding them into the discovery of forms of worship which are satisfying to them.

Material and form should be varied enough that the children may choose those which best meet their need. An evaluation of worship materials would include such questions as, Does it embody the right idea of God? Are all the ideas that it contains consistent with a Christian attitude toward life? Is it worth while from the standpoint of literary and artistic merit? Is it within the vocabulary and the emotional capacity of primary children? It is evident, of course, that

---

[1] *Then I Think of God*, by Mabel A. Niedermeyer; *Tell Me About God*, by Mary Alice Jones; *God's Wonder World*, by Bernice Bryant.

the leader who is to use these standards in the selection of material must herself have a Christian experience and philosophy of life that will enable her to decide the first two questions, she must have discriminating taste that will enable her to answer the third, and she must have a knowledge of primary children that will make it possible for her to judge its suitability as implied in the fourth question.

THE MATERIALS OF WORSHIP

An important function of the leader of the Primary Department is that of bringing within the experience of the children certain materials which they can use in worship. It is important that these shall not take the place of the children's own informal expression of their love and gratitude, of their joy in a sense of companionship with God. A song or a prayer may help the child to say what he feels, but lacks the skill to say. Unless the song or prayer does say what the child wishes to say, the use of it does not become worship for him. Singing and praying have become such customary things for children, as well as adults, that they frequently become meaningless. Yet the deepest and richest religious experiences are frequently associated with a hymn or other devotional material.

Children's songs. It is a long way in more than years from Isaac Watts' *Divine and Moral Songs for Children,* to the songs which are part of the worship in a Primary Department today. While we honor that author of some of the great hymns of the church, we would not wish to return to the singing of a hymn which contained such a stanza as this:

> Then let me join this holy train,
> And my first offering bring;
> The eternal God will not disdain
> To hear an infant sing.

It is much more consistent with our conception of God and of a child's religion, to teach:

> When I am happiest I sing,
> Or else a little prayer I say
> To God, who gives me everything,
> To God, who loves me every day.[2]

---

[2]Danielson and Conant, *Song and Play for Children.* Copyright Pilgrim Press. Used by permission.

There are rich sources from which to choose what we shall bring into the experiences of the children. The songs of the Primary Department will include not only songs of worship but of fellowship and right living. One should be sure, however, that the number which one selects includes an adequate selection of hymns of worship suitable for children. The limitations of time are such that probably not more than twenty-four songs will be included in the list used during the year by any one department. These would be extended over a period of eighteen months or more and would constitute the songs with which the children became familiar during their three years in the Primary Department. Great care must therefore be exercised that only the best shall be included and that the children shall be helped to find the greatest possible satisfaction in the expression of their religious feeling through song. Nothing trivial or lacking in beauty should be offered to them. Such hymns as "All Things Bright and Beautiful" and "All People That on Earth Do Dwell" should find a place in the worship experiences of all children.

Children's prayers. Perhaps no form of prayer can ever say exactly what the one who is praying really feels and would like to say to God, his Father. Certainly children should be given every opportunity for formulating their own prayers and for suggesting what the leader shall include in the prayers she offers as the common prayer of the whole group. Prayers of beautiful simplicity have been made by children and their religious experiences have been enriched thereby.

The practice of having children offer public prayer involves a good many dangers. There is always the possibility that it will become a performance rather than a prayer and that the child will be conscious of the effect he is producing rather than having a genuine religious experience. But sometimes the atmosphere and the situation are just right and children spontaneously pray aloud, as members of the group. Such occasions probably come more frequently in the smaller groups, but the wise leader will be sensitive to the readiness of the children to pray, individually, in their own way, when she is sure that the situation is right.

Sometimes children will find in a poem or a collection of prayers, something that they would like to say. One Primary leader read to the children some of the prayers in *First Prayers for Children.*[3] She simply told them that this was a book of prayers that some men, who remembered when they were children and who were friends of children now, had written. The children chose one or two that she read and asked to learn them. Several of them asked for copies of the prayer, "One Saturday Morning," and said that they would like to learn it and use it as their own prayer. The whole group wanted to learn one of the prayers to pray in the morning.

At another time when prayers from the same collection were read to the children, they suggested writing prayers of their own and they cooperated in writing several. Copies of these were written on the blackboard or given to the children to take home and they were later included in the worship service of the department. Some of the children wrote prayers at home and brought them to the session.

Such verse or song prayers as "Father, We Thank Thee for the Night," may be used very effectively if they are not used so continuously that they become meaningless. It is not an exaggeration to say that there are Primary Departments in which a verse or song of this kind is used every Sunday for a period of years. Of necessity it becomes a mere repetition of words.

The use of the Lord's Prayer in the Primary Department presents difficulty because the younger children, in fact most of the children in the department, not only do not understand it but they misunderstand it, which is a more serious matter. Probably some time before the children leave the department, they will become familiar with this prayer in connection with the work of the second or third grade. They will be prepared to join with others in the church service or when they go into the Junior Department, in praying this great prayer which Jesus taught his disciples, and it will have much more meaning for them if they know something of its significance before they memorize the words. The fact that some children have learned the words by rote either in the church school or the public school, when they could not understand them, has been a hindrance to their appreciation of that great prayer of the church.

[3]John Oxenham and Roderic Dunkerley.

Even in the simplest material for children there will sometimes be words or phrases that should be explained and discussed. If we were to use only the vocabulary which the child acquires through his public school, home, and community experience, there are certain words which they would never have as part of their own working vocabulary. Even the word "worship" itself is not a word that is familiar to children and yet is one which they need. Occasionally time may be given in the department session, apart from the worship service itself, to talk about some of these things. One leader wrote the word "worship" on the blackboard and guided the children as they discovered its meaning. Even a simple phrase such as "He cares for me," in the lovely hymn by that name, needs to be talked about, or the children may get the idea that God in some mysterious way surrounds them and protects them from danger, while the real meaning is to be found in "caring" in the sense of being interested in, and loving. Beautiful hymns and prayers should not be picked to pieces and the beauty of their message marred by too much discussion, but an understanding leader can guide children into the true and deeper meaning of the songs and prayers they use.

Scripture material. Children enjoy having the Bible read to them, especially the dignified and beautiful things to be found in the psalms. One day as a leader was reading quietly and reverently some selections from Psalm 104, a child in the group said, "That's talking to God, isn't it?" Then the leader stopped and they talked about the psalms, how they were used by people who were worshiping God, and the children found great satisfaction in learning a portion of the psalm she had read and using it as a prayer.

Frequently the children will discover that some of the verses or longer passages that they learn, which are connected with what they may be doing in their class groups, are prayers or are ways of talking and thinking about God. One child was much interested in the prayer book which he saw in the home of a Roman Catholic friend. He told about it at the church school and the group decided to make a book of prayers for their department. They chose hymns, Bible verses, psalms, poems, which were prayers and had these copied in a large book which they made of heavy paper. They decorated the book with pictures of lovely things in the world of nature and on the outside they placed a copy of Millet's "The Angelus."

The offering service. The experience of giving includes not only worship but fellowship for it is something that we do together. However, it usually finds a place as part of the worship service of the Primary Department. It should not become mechanical or too formal, and yet children love ritual, and when they plan their own offering service they are inclined to make it dignified and orderly. Perhaps the schedule of the session is such that it is best for the children to leave their offering as they enter the room. The basket may later be brought to the table at the front of the room when the offertory prayer or song provides the dedication of the gifts. The song should be worthy of the occasion; such a song as "Thy Work, O God, Needs Many Hands."[1]

It will also be necessary, of course, to find another time when the children may plan for the use of their gifts of money, and discover how the budget of the church and school is administered.

WHAT ENVIRONMENT IS MOST CONDUCIVE TO WORSHIP?

If the leader would be seated with the group of children when they are assembled for worship, it would create the feeling of a shared experience in which leaders and children are approaching their common Father. If the group is large the leader will perhaps sit on a chair that is higher than those of the children, although this is not necessary.

The personal element. The crudest surroundings can be made a place of worship if all the people who are there are worshipful. If the teachers or the assistants feel that the primary session does not offer them an opportunity for worship, but that they must seek a different sort of place and occasion for their own worship experiences, this will detract from the effectiveness of the whole environment. Even when they are willing to "set a good example" and participate in the session, the lack of reality is apparent to themselves and to the children.

---

[1] *Hymns for Primary Worship.*

The primary leader who has reached that point where she can find a worship service with the children, a deep and inspiring religious experience will be richly rewarded.

How far apart adults and children sometimes are in the service of worship is apparent when the leader prays for the children and about them instead of realizing that she is attempting to voice the prayer of the whole group of which she and the children and the teachers are all members.

A child's love of order and ritual. While it is quite true that worship may often be informal and spontaneous, it must not be forgotten that children love order and ritual. When a group of children plan, as they may do sometimes, a service of worship in which they will ask the other children to share, it is interesting to note the extensive use they make of as much form and ritual as is familiar to them. A group of children were having a meeting for such a purpose in an informal period and these are some of the things they said (selected from a full report of their discussion): "How will we get everybody to be still and think, so they will be ready to pray?" "Let's have Miss Eleanor (the pianist) play something that sounds like praying, like the organ does in church!" "How will we let them know when to stand up and sit down at the right time?" "What can we put in the front to help make things beautiful?" "Can we say our psalm well enough that it will sound as important as it really is?" These are evidences of a striving for order, form, impressiveness, in which children find satisfaction.

Room arrangement. Children respond favorably to beauty and order although they may not know why. They also like best the situations to which they have contributed something. Therefore whether it is a room used only for worship, or one used for many other activities, or only a corner, it should be a place which helps children to worship. Colorfulness, sunshine, the beauty of flowers or growing things, helps to create a happy environment. The soft glow of candlelight is also beautiful and if candles are not used for symbolism they are as suitable as flowers or a picture. Chairs in orderly arrangement reduce confusion and help to create the atmosphere for a worship experience. Children may have a share in all of these arrangements and grow in their appreciation of the experience of worship.

SUGGESTIONS FOR FURTHER STUDY AND DISCUSSION

1. Plan a "worship center" for a Primary room, indicating the arrangement of furniture and the provision for beauty and quiet.

2. How would you plan the environment to bring about an appreciation of the wonders in God's world, leading to worship?

3. Study and evaluate ten songs in a book of children's songs, according to the idea of God they contain, their Christian attitude, their literary and artistic merit, and their suitability for children as to vocabulary and ideas.

4. Read several children's prayers to a child or group of children and note their comments or attitude.

Chapter VIII

THE WORLD OF PRIMARY CHILDREN

PRELIMINARY OBSERVATION

1. Find out what international and interracial contacts the children in your group have through persons, books, travel, and other resources.

2. Discover and make a list of the groups of people in your own city or community whose needs the children may have a share in meeting or with whom they may work.

3. What race or class prejudices would have to be taken into account in planning the service activities of the primary children in your church?

4. What sources of information concerning the missionary work of your church are available? What provision is made for children to share in this work?

THE PRIMARY CHILD'S EXPANDING WORLD

A child's world is made up of all the places, persons, things of which he is aware. His attitude toward them is of the greatest importance. It reveals his character and in turn molds and changes it. Christian education must take into account a child's relationships with his world, for many of its aims can be accomplished only through these relationships.

What a child thinks about other people, how he feels about them, are part of his personal development and of his Christian growth. Friendliness, goodwill, appreciation, expressed in relation to all kinds of people are the beginning of the attitude we call "world mindedness" in a more mature Christian. His attitudes toward his possessions are helping to set a pattern for his stewardship in years to come. If he feels responsible for the care of the things that are his, if he enjoys sharing them with others, he is growing toward Christian stewardship. If he enjoys having things other children do not have and in keeping them exclusively for his own use, the church faces the problem of helping him change these fundamental attitudes, if Christian love and service are to grow. Providing experiences of sharing and giving through which a

child finds as great satisfaction as in a sense of personal possession is probably the only way the change can be brought
about.

Let us think first of his relationships with other people, as
they are planned and provided by the church.

FELLOWSHIP IN WORK

The enjoyment children find in doing things together in
the Primary Department is best described as "fellowship."
It is a conscious, purposeful working together. Group activity is valuable quite as much for this quality of fellowship as
for the work accomplished. Children who work together in
the care and arrangement of their room at the church and in
making it beautiful can find happiness and satisfaction in the
companionship while doing it as well as in the orderly, beautiful room. Two ten-year-old boys looked into the primary
room early one Sunday morning. Of course they had attained the greatly advanced stage of being juniors, but they
did remember some things about their primary experiences.
Some of the primary children were busy in their room. One
junior said, "Do you remember the time we fixed up that
whole picture file and got everything straightened out so the
kids and even the teachers could find things? Boy! That
was keen, wasn't it?" "Yeh, and we had fun, too!" his
friend replied. What did they remember? The fun of doing
something important together.

FELLOWSHIP IN PERSONAL EXPERIENCES

Sometimes the element of fellowship in the Primary Department has been thought of in terms of the birthday service
and the greetings which are extended to the new pupils and
visitors. These are properly an expression of fellowship and
certainly have their place in the procedures of a Primary Department. But it is essential that there shall be in these courtesies a feeling of sincere friendliness and desire to express it.
The shy visitor or new child who suffers when he is asked
to stand before the department while the children address a
song to him, is hardly having an experience of fellowship.
The child who is pleased with the personal recognition of his
birthday, who enjoys being in the spotlight and who likes the
experience of dropping his money in a penny at a time while

it is counted, but knows nothing about the cause for which the money is to go, does not find fellowship in the experience.

Recognition of birthdays. A child's birthday is such an important thing in his own eyes and gives him such satisfaction, that quite naturally his friends share in the celebration of it. Each birthday marks great advancement in the mind of the child, and sometimes new privileges, such as staying up a half-hour longer in the evening or having a room of his own, are attained along with the birthday. Usually there are gifts and sometimes a party. All in all, a birthday is a self-centered sort of experience, and probably it is right that it should be so. It is right also that he shall feel that his friends in the Primary Department, the children, the teachers and the leaders, are interested in this important occasion in his life. Because of the limited time for many Primary Department sessions, it is usually desirable to have this celebration of birthdays one Sunday in each month. The birthday letter or card which comes addressed to the child and is delivered by the postman is a cherished possession.

The motive for the birthday service and birthday offering needs to be made quite clear if the experience is to be valuable to the child. The offering is a way of sharing our happiness with others, and it is a way of saying, "Thank you," to God our Father, for his love and care. The birthday greeting which the children may sing or say is their opportunity for saying to their friend that they are glad he is having the happiness of a birthday. But the experience becomes most meaningful when God is included in it through the prayer verse or a simple prayer offered by the leader. The church may help the child to find a religious experience in connection with his birthday.

The service must be very simple and brief. It would seem that cake, real or imitation, might be left to the home and other experiences to provide. Symbolism is often confusing to a child, but the lighted candles, growing more numerous each year, seem to provide a simple picture of growth and, if the symbolism is not pressed to the point of insisting on the significance of the light, the beauty of the candlelight would seem to justify its use. Some departments have found pleasure and satisfaction in the use of the Hanukkah lamp, which is used in the celebration of the Jewish Feast of Lights. It has nine candle sockets which makes it possible to use it for all of the birthdays in the Primary Department. The fact that the Feast of Lights, with its lighting of an additional candle for each of the days of the feast, was kept in Jesus' home when he was a little boy, gives added value to the lamp in the eyes of the children. The Feast of Lights comes late in December and includes the day when Christians celebrate the birthday of Jesus. Since the lamp is used reverently in this way, it does not seem to be an unfair use of the materials of another religious faith. In fact, it will increase a sense of fellowship with Jewish children. A rabbi who was asked how he felt when he saw the Hanukkah lamp used in this way by a group of Christian children said, "It warmed my heart to see the little lamp used by them!" The story of the Feast of Lights will be found in a dictionary of the Bible and may be told to the children without going into the details of the restoration of the Temple, which the feast celebrates.

Celebrating other happy occasions. Birthdays need not be the only occasion for celebration in the Primary Department. When Margaret's father came back from the long business trip to South America, when Jack's much-loved grandmother came to live with them, when Dick's mother who had been ill so long came home from the hospital and the family was re-united once more, all of these events were occasions for re-joicing on the part of the other children and the teachers and leaders in the Primary Department. They were mentioned in the worship and fellowship of the day, they reminded the children of certain songs or Bible verses that they loved.

Local congregations have their special anniversaries. Very often these are days which the children can share in celebrating. Young as they are, children revel in reminiscences. A certain congregation had been meeting for a long time in rented halls and buildings. The day that they assembled for the first time in their new building was a time of great re-joicing. A movie was made of some of the departments of the school as they went into their room or began their work. Each year, thereafter, the church celebrated this day and the children thoroughly enjoyed seeing the picture, in some of which they appeared as little children. The church became dearer to them each year with the celebration and they found satisfaction in new gifts for it and in making it beautiful. Best of all, the children grew in a sense of "belonging" which is essential to all fellowship.

Expressions of courtesy. The practice of having new pupils and visitors who have come into a strange environment, come to the front of the room while the other children sing a song of greeting, presents a number of difficulties. The shy child does not enjoy it, and yet to make a distinction between different children is puzzling to the other children. Probably the wisest plan is simply to mention the names of those who are new pupils in the department or visiting it and let the song of greeting be sung without making the strangers too conspicuous for their own comfort. A department may have a committee of children, with one teacher as a member, who will report the names of the new pupils or child visitors. Or the secretary may be asked to bring this information, thus relating her and her work to the fellowship of the group. It must always be kept in mind that the purpose is to let these new friends know that the others are glad they have come, and to help them become members of the group as quickly as possible.

Fellowship is part of every situation in the Primary Department. It enters into worship, it is part of the work in which the children engage, it enters into all of the learning experiences which the children are having. More than that, it will carry them out beyond the four walls of their department room and the church building itself, as they establish contact with other members of God's great family and share in carrying on his work in the world.

WIDER RELATIONSHIPS

How do children establish relationships with the world beyond their personal contacts? In the newly acquired ability to read, books take on new importance. The pictures in books mean more because of the words that go with them. The people in books become more real. It is sometimes not easy for a child to think at once whether a certain person he recalls was a much loved character in a book or a flesh-and-blood neighbor. The multitude of colorful books about life in every land on earth have a large part in peopling a child's world with persons quite unlike themselves but vastly interesting. Country children meet city children, city children visit the country, racial lines are crossed, all on the pages of a child's story book.

Airplane travel is not an uncommon experience, real or book-wise, among primary children and they can easily imagine dropping down on almost any country in the world. Magic carpets sound very inefficient these days! Automobile touring has brought families in touch with many ways of living.

Movies, and the radio, and television bring other lands into the world of children, all too often in the wake or vanguard of war. Children are reasonably familiar with places and people which were unknown to children—or to many adults— a few years ago. A globe means something to children younger than heretofore.

Sometimes there are children in the department who have been in other countries, or members or friends of their families have been. In one community which did not include many people of wealth or high position, it was discovered, through the preparation of an exhibit, that there were more than a dozen children who had, through their homes, international contacts. All of this means that the children are acquiring attitudes toward the people of other lands and offers an opportunity for Christian interpretation. Nor do we need to wait for personal contacts of this kind. It is within the functions of the church to supply them. Through the books on the reading table, the pictures which the children find on the table or in the file, the stories they hear, the missionary who visits the church, interests are stimulated and friendly feelings aroused.

How attitudes develop. What children think about these lands and the people in them is more important than the amount of detailed information they have. Facts are important but feelings about those facts are more important, for feelings determine what one does about the facts. It is essential that feelings of good will, of friendliness, of concern for those who need help, shall keep pace with a child's growing knowledge of the world. These feelings can only develop through exercise and they must be completely free from condescension.

Discovering needs. Sometimes a situation near at hand presents an opportunity for growth in understanding. A family of Displaced Persons came to live in a certain community, sponsored by a church that provided a home for them. Of course the women of the church were active in providing household furnishings, the men did the necessary repairs, the young people provided pictures and other decorative items. The committee almost forgot to give the children of the church any share in the enterprise, although there were children in the family. An alert children's worker talked with the leaders and then with the children. The investigation and planning, which resulted in picture books, dolls and other toys finding their place in the home for the new family, gave the children at least a small amount of understanding of some world problems and ways they are being faced. It would have been unfortunate if the committee had thoughtlessly deprived the children of such a worth-while experience.

In another community there was a colony of Mexicans who lived in temporary quarters, because the fathers were engaged in doing work on the railroad. There were children in the colony. One child reported to his church school class this discovery, which an aunt of his had first told him about, and the children discussed the situation. They decided that probably there were some things which the Mexican children did not have because they were not living in their own homes. Incidentally, there was no feeling of condescension, for the primary children thought this would be a very interesting way to live, although it might have certain disadvantages. They thought perhaps the little children would like some toys, perhaps the older ones would enjoy some books. What kind of books? They decided it would be best to ask Fred's aunt to find out if the people could read English, especially the children. It was discovered that they could not, so pictures were decided upon as being better than books, for, as one child said, "Anybody knows what a picture means." The further investigation by Fred's aunt revealed the fact that there was one child who was ill, so fruit and flowers were decided upon as suitable gifts for her. Christmas gifts were planned and delivered in a delightfully mysterious way.

The primary graded lessons of every denomination include units of work and study which are designed particularly to open doors to better understanding of people with whom the children do not have direct personal contact. These are usually considered missionary units. Such studies are essential in helping children to understand the nature of God, his love for all people, his desire that they shall know and love him. They are part of any beginning understanding of the Gospel and its message of love and they are also needed as the children become better acquainted with the life and work of the church. There are, in addition to these basic units, other missionary books and activities which are part of co-operative Protestantism. They should be fitted into the church's ongoing program for children, not considered something apart. In fact missionary education must always be an integral part of a total program and not an additional item which may or may not be included or which calls for an additional organization.

The attractive world friendship books which appear each year can be enjoyed in the home, read aloud, and treasured on the children's book shelves. The suggestions for projects can be carried out by families as well as church groups. They should also find their place on the reading table in relation to units of work in the lesson courses.

Problems and difficulties. Whether the home or the church provided the opportunities for service to other groups, there are certain difficulties involved which cannot be overlooked, or we shall defeat the purpose and narrow the children's fellowship rather than extend it. For example, if there is a very strong prejudice against a certain race, this prejudice cannot be overcome by having the more favored children send a gift to the less fortunate ones. In fact, snobbishness and a sense of superiority may be developed by just such a procedure. If opportunities for first-hand contact between children of different groups are arranged, it may result in so much opposition on the part of the parents that the children become aware of and share in a prejudice of which they had not been conscious before that time. If this occurs, it will be increasingly difficult to overcome this prejudice in the future.

There is the danger also of exploiting the very persons whose needs we are attempting to help the children discover and meet. A group of Italian children were invited to a certain church to a party, given by the Primary Department.

The guests did not understand the situation. The procedure and the games and the refreshments were all unlike the things with which they were familiar. Altogether it was a very unhappy experience for them and certainly no broadening of sympathy and fellowship resulted for anyone. One's heart goes out, also, to the groups of orphans who are frequently taken about to different churches in order to create interest in the work of the orphanage. On one such occasion the children of the Primary Department provided refreshments in a very condescending sort of way. The orphans sang some songs and gave a few recitations. The utmost care was taken that the two groups of children should not mingle in any sort of close personal contact. From every viewpoint of Christian fellowship the experience was a bad one for all the children concerned.

Meeting the problems. Shall we, therefore, do nothing, except perhaps to let the children engage in a few harmless and benign activities which are not likely to involve too many problems? Shall we contribute to the continuance of social injustice by not calling it to the attention of the children, or shall we say perhaps that these are problems which they will have to face later? Is there nothing that the leader of primary children may do to extend the fellowship of the children and to broaden their sympathy?

We cannot ignore the fact that children are inevitably caught in whatever economic or social situations prevail in the communities in which they live. Children are forming opinions, and judgments, which are largely a reflection of those expressed by their parents and other adult relatives and friends. Whether the children's leader in the church considers these opinions right or not, they must be recognized as factors which cannot be ignored in any effort to lead the children as far as possible in the direction of clear thinking and right attitudes.

First of all, the leader herself must be a person who is intelligently and sympathetically concerned about the social order of our time and keenly sensitive to social injustice of any kind. However limited the world of a child may be, that of the teacher of children must be unlimited. Her interest and sympathy must be broad and informed. In fact, strong class antagonism or race prejudices would handicap the leader of children to such an extent that she should diligently try to discover if they are there and set about ridding herself of them immediately. Sometimes they are the result of tradition and environment, but thoughtful study can overcome these influences and enable one to outgrow them.

In any case of need which grows out of physical limitation, social injustice or race prejudice, the leader of children may ask herself, "Is this a need which children can understand? Can they help to meet it? Will their sympathy and fellowship be increased?"

When these three questions can be answered in the affirmative the leader must make it possible for the children to get in touch with persons who thoroughly understand the situation and are working intelligently in it. Of course, there are certain very simple situations in which the children may make first-hand investigation of everything that they need to know but if it goes outside their usual circle of experience, they will probably need expert advice. For example, the children who planned for the happiness of the Mexican children, got in touch, through the aunt of the little boy who brought the information, with the Americanization section of a social service organization in their city. This enabled them to be tactful in their approach and to discover what was needed. This would not have been possible if a group of children and their teachers had gone directly to the Mexican colony and attempted to make the investigation themselves. The other procedure also gave the children fellowship with those who were doing social service work in their city.

Perhaps some of the needs the children themselves discover will not be so remote from an adult standpoint. In a roundabout way a group of primary children learned of a little girl who lived in an adjoining state and who for three months or longer every year was entirely shut off from the little church and public school that she attended, because of bad roads. They wrote her letters, sent booklets containing all of their story papers, sent her a scrapbook of stories and pictures and began a friendship which extended throughout the year. At Christmas time she sent to the Primary Department a box of Christmas greens, which meant quite as much to those dwellers in city apartments as anything that they had sent to her could possibly mean. They made their room beautiful with her gift and then arranged to have the greens sent to a children's hospital where they could be enjoyed again.

INTERCHANGE OF GIFTS AND HELP

Fellowship is always a two-way experience. The children who had received the Christmas greens from the little girl in the country had a richer experience in fellowship than if the giving had been all on one side. When the little Mexican girl who was ill sent a picture that she had drawn of the flowers that the children sent her, the relationship became a more friendly one.

It is equally true that when children can join with other groups in carrying forward some enterprise, the experience of fellowship is more valuable than when one group performs a service for the other. It is by working with people that we come to know them and to make friends with them. If the children from the orphanage had been invited to come and have a real party with the children in the department described, if they had been asked to be responsible for certain things in the party, such as planning some of the games, if both groups could have joined in serving the refreshments and in other activities connected with the party, the experience would have been a valuable one. The guests would have become just "other children" instead of "orphans." Whenever it is possible for children of different races to join in carrying out some plan, the experience becomes more valuable than when the one group serves the other or even when there is an interchange of gifts. The democracy of childhood would quite easily make all of this possible if it were not for the prejudices of adults which are passed on to the children.

It is especially important that in giving money children shall have feelings of friendliness and good will entirely free from any feeling of superiority. Nothing could be worse than the glib way in which some children talk about bringing their offering for "the poor children." Probably the money does as much good but certainly the giver does not have a religious experience unless love and appreciation accompany his gift.

Primary children have had enough arithmetic that they understand and will be interested in the amount which the children give for the work of the local church and for the missionary work. They are interested in the different things for which the church must spend its money. Too much detail would be beyond their skill in reading figures, but they can get a very clear idea of the general plan of caring for the expenses of the church. They can know something of the share which the Primary Department may have in this. They have a sense of fellowship in the life and work of the church by feeling that they share in providing for it. They can know how the missionary money of the church is given, the different things which are supported by it. Their giving may be an experience in a world-wide fellowship through their church.

FELLOWSHIP WITH GOD

It does not require any repetition of religious phrases or forms for children to have a genuine sense of fellowship with God as they find themselves working for and with other children who are part of his family. Not merely the fact that the work begins and perhaps is carried on in connection with the Primary Department of the church, but the spirit in which it is done and the attitude of the leaders will help to make the activities in which the children engage fruitful in Christian world citizenship.

SUGGESTIONS FOR FURTHER STUDY AND DISCUSSION

1. Discover and list the international contacts of a group of primary children and note those which offer opportunity for the extension of the children's fellowship through the church school.

2. Review the list of race and class prejudices referred to in the second "Preliminary Observation" at the beginning of this chapter and plan what procedures you would use to guide the children's experiences so that these might be overcome or the way at least opened for new knowledge or sympathy in relation to them.

3. If the children use expressions like "dago," "nigger," "chink," how would you seek to correct this?

4. Study the outlines or textbooks of the lesson materials used in your school to discover the suggestions given there for study and activities that will broaden the children's fellowship. These will probably not be labeled "missionary" but the material and statement of desired outcomes will reveal their purpose.

Chapter IX

DEPARTMENT ADMINISTRATION

Preliminary Observation

1. Analyze the work of a Primary Department by making a list of the things which must be done (a) in preparation during the week; (b) immediately in advance of the session; (c) during the session. Indicate in which of these you think children should share.

2. What seems to be the division of responsibility among the officers and teachers? Is this division so complete that the work of the department lacks unity?

3. Do administrative details, such as records, reports, announcements, intrude upon the work of the department? Or do they contribute to it?

It may seem that this chapter should have come first in a book on the subject of administration. If the work of the department were to be made to fit a plan of administration, it should of course be studied first. But the reverse is true. Administration must fit the situation, the plan of organization, the time and space available, the opportunities for children to worship and to work together. When these have been explored and decisions made as to the best procedure in a particular department, then administration can be planned and carried out. Good administration is good management. The more successful it is, the less it is in evidence. Administration really consists of keeping all persons, materials, time schedules, activities in proper relationship to each other so that all of them may make their contribution to the ongoing work. For example, unless teaching materials are available at the right time, they will not serve their purpose. Good administration will see to it that all such materials are on hand ahead of the time they are to be used.

Unless accurate attendance records are kept, and use made of them after they are compiled, boys and girls may be neglected because they were not followed up promptly, the causes of absence discovered and overcome, when possible. Good administration will be concerned not only with keeping accurate records but with using them.

116

Often a primary superintendent will say, "I would much rather teach." But the atmosphere in which learning and worship takes place is in itself a form of teaching and only good administration can make it what it should be. There is in some primary groups an unfortunate line of division between the work of the superintendent or leading teacher and the class teachers. Of course there must be a division of responsibility but all the workers in a department must feel concerned for the success of the work each one does. Nothing could be more artificial than a situation in which the department superintendent is responsible for the children's assembly for worship and fellowship but has no opportunity to participate in the work of class groups or even to know what is done there; while teachers feel no responsibility for the department session even to the extent of entering into it, feeling that the worship is "for the children." Good administration will bring about a unity of planning and purpose throughout the work of the department.

Let us look at the aspects of the work of a Primary Department which require administration. No list would fit every situation but many details will be neglected unless the workers in each department have a common understanding of the work which must be done and the allocation of responsibility.

RESPONSIBILITIES OF WORKERS

Certain administrative duties are cared for in connection with the session of the department, others must be looked after at other times. One of the weaknesses of many departments is that too many administrative details are crowded into a brief session. The superintendent and officers are so busy looking after details that the joy and purpose of the session are obscured, because the leaders are not free to enter into teaching situations.

The department superintendent. The usual division of work in a Primary Department is that the superintendent or leading teacher shall be responsible for the room and equipment, for such portions of the session as when the entire department is together, for securing the necessary supplies and working materials, for maintaining a staff of teachers and officers, planning and conducting workers' conferences, for supervising the work of the department, helping to maintain the attendance (a responsibility in which the teachers share), serving as the point of contact between the Primary Department and the other departments of the school and church life. But it must be remembered that the superintendent is more than an administrative officer. She is a teacher who guides and shares in important learning experiences.

The teachers. The teachers (assistants, in the single grade or department unit plan) are responsible for work done in the class or groups, for keeping up the attendance in their groups, and for maintaining contact with the children's life during the week. Too often this division of responsibility works against the unity of the whole program. One person is "in charge" during the assembly and others during the periods of group work. Certainly the teachers and assistants are concerned in all of the activities which center in the department room. Their interest will be evident in the way in which they participate in these activities. They will be responsible for guiding and initiating as well as sharing them.

The secretary. The marking of attendance, the making of the weekly report to the general secretary of the school, the filling out of enrollment cards are only the routine duties of a secretary. She is a member of the group who may share in many of its activities, and who is looked upon by the children as a friend and helper. It is necessary for her to know the ideals and objectives of the department, to be familiar with the working materials, to attend all of the department conferences. She must know how to be efficient and inconspicuous, and to look upon her work as an important part of the educational process.

The pianist. An intelligent adjustability is as essential to a good pianist in the Primary Department as is musical skill. This involves a knowledge of the purposes and plans of the department and the ability to fit into a program which may change to suit the interests and needs of the child. She will be so familiar with all the source materials, songbooks, looseleaf collections of songs, instrumental selections, that she can make them available whenever they are needed.

Shared experiences. When the department is organized according to the single grade plan and each grade has its own complete session and room it will, of course, be necessary for the primary superintendent or supervisor to work with the teachers at times other than the session, in order to bring about unity of spirit and purpose. But when the different grades and classes of the department join in experiences of fellowship and worship and in certain activities, it is of the greatest importance that all of these experiences shall be shared by teachers, children, and leaders. The experiences of worship should be shared by teachers as well as children, and all of them enter into the joys of fellowship and the activities essential to the work of the department.

This sharing of experience will come as the result of having a share in purposing and planning what shall be done, both in workers' conferences and in the freest discussion in which children, teachers, and leaders will share.

The superintendent will make possible this full participation on the part of all the adult leaders in the department by being skillful in coordinating all the activities in the department whether they begin in a small group or class, or arise in the larger group. This must be done without thwarting the purposes of any group. She may become aware of these group activities through some question or request which a child brings to her, or through the information the teacher gives her, either in advance of the session or during the session if the activity has been spontaneous and unforeseen. She may even discover it as she observes the different groups and shares in their work. All of this she will weave into the unity of the session as she guides the worship and conversation of the larger group. On the other hand, as interests and plans develop in the larger group, she will relate these to the work of the classes or interest groups, and make it possible for the children to work together purposefully.

What children may do. Quite as important as the part that teachers will have in planning the equipment and program of the department, will be the share that children may have. Children much prefer doing real things that need to be done rather than carrying on the pseudo-child projects which we so often set up for them. When the administrative work of a department is analyzed, it is surprising how many of the different things that have to be done can be done by children and are educationally profitable in the doing.

One primary superintendent always arrived forty-five minutes early and had every poster, picture, flower and book in place before a child arrived. One morning she was delayed and the usual preparations in the room had to be done in a very short time and all of the children who were there helped. It was such fun and the children were full of ideas and suggestions, as well as energy! It is true the table at the front of the room was not quite as perfect in its arrangement, a seasonal poster did not seem to be in exactly the right spot, and one or two other things were not entirely satisfactory to the adult eye. But in the children's eyes they were quite perfect. One little girl, giving a last fond pat to the table cover said rather wistfully, "I wish you'd be late every Sunday, and I could always fix this table."

The superintendent found her program modified by the experiences they had shared in preparing the room together. They sang about the church and thanked God, their Father, that they had one. They talked about churches everywhere and about some people who wanted one but didn't have it. They planned ways of sharing their church and lovely things that they could do for it. That superintendent and the teachers decided that the children cared very much more for something they had helped to make than for something that was made ready for them, and the experience of preparing the room was a shared experience from that time. The superintendent came no less early, but the preparations she made were those which would make the activities and the experiences of the children of the greatest value.

Arranging the room, making it beautiful, getting out working materials, are only the beginning of administrative duties in which children may share. Third-grade children are quite capable of sorting the story papers. The library or browsing table can be planned and arranged and cared for by children. Many varied activities which arise in the class groups will relate themselves to matters of department administration such as the seasonal decoration of the room, planning a program, writing letters to absent friends, planning for visitors. These are all part of the life of the department.

Administration that merely gets things done may be efficient, but it is of greater value when it becomes an experience in Christian living, shared by children and their adult friends and leaders.

RECORDS

Records are valuable, not so much in the making of them as in the use that is made of them. Probably there are vast quantities of church school records that are without value because no use is made of them. They are kept as a matter of habit. Sometimes certain items on which information is desired in the older departments are imposed upon the younger children as well, for the sake of uniformity. The records of a church school are the most vital kind of "human accounting" and should enable the educational leaders of the church to know whether or not they are doing a satisfactory piece of work, that satisfaction to be measured according to the needs and capacity of the various ages in the school.

Record of a session. This record may be in the form of notes or a diary. It should be made very soon after the session, in fact certain notes may be made at the time of the session. It may be made by the superintendent (the teacher in the single grade plan) or by an assistant who is responsible for it. It is very desirable to have stenographic records made occasionally, for a period of six weeks, and made again at intervals.

All such reports would include a record of the procedures, the situations out of which they came, the projects that were being carried on, the materials that were used, the comments of the children, evidences of their attitude, problems these revealed, as well as facts such as weather, the number present, and any unusual circumstances.

Such records may be used in planning future sessions, in measuring the achievement of the department or group, and in setting up new objectives.

Enrollment. There are at least three other types of records which the Primary Department will wish to keep. The first is the enrollment of the children. It is not always easy to secure the accurate enrollment of a child of primary age. It is also difficult to know whether a child is a new pupil or a visitor. Sometimes a child will say that he is coming to the school, "all the time," when he is there for a month's visit. If a child comes alone or is accompanied by another child, it may be necessary to get in touch with the home for further information. But the enrollment should be accurate and complete, including the child's full name, that of his parents, the address and telephone number, the date of his birth (including the year), his grade at school and the school building, when the children come from more than one school district, and the church affiliations of the parents.

In some schools it is the custom to make only a temporary enrollment when a child first comes to the school and to transfer this to a permanent enrollment card when he has been present three successive Sundays. Of course, there would be exceptions to such a rule when it was known that the family had moved into the community and were entering into the church life. One secretary was so completely bound by the system of enrolling on the third Sunday that she made only a temporary enrollment of the little daughter of their new pastor! At such time as the enrollment is complete and permanent, a duplicate should be sent to the enrollment file of the school. It is better to have a child enrolled in the Primary Department than in a general enrollment office, for the officers in the Primary Department will in this way be enabled to establish a personal relation that is even more important than the information on the enrollment card.

To avoid the danger of having a child spend two or three Sundays in the wrong group and the difficulty of making a change later, it is desirable that the temporary enrollment shall be made the first Sunday that he attends, unless it is known that he is only a visitor.

The teacher will wish to have her own record of the child, including all the information on the enrollment card and much in addition which she will discover through her contact with the child. This will include information concerning the number in the family, ages of brothers and sisters, and general home conditions.

Weekly record of attendance. A second form of record will be the weekly record of attendance and possibly of punctuality. This record must usually be made out quite early in the session so that it may be sent to the general secretary of the school in time for him to compile the day's report. This attendance record should be made with the least possible interruption of the department's activities. The manner in which it is made will be determined by the arrangement of the building, to some extent. For example, in the case of the department meeting in one large room, the secretary could

compile such a report as this by merely sitting at her desk
and observing the class groups. Even if the groups meet in
rooms immediately adjoining, if the children pass by the secretary's desk, she may mark the attendance record. If the
secretary cannot make this record, the teacher or an assistant
should make available to the secretary of the department
such facts as the number present, the number of visitors, and
the number who were on time. She should be able to do this
without taking the time and attention of the group. This
information can be placed outside the door, in some recep-
tacle, and the secretary can secure it in this way. The marking of the individual child's record of attendance may be
made after the session by the teacher or by an assistant during the session. In the single grade plan of organization or
the department unit plan, the secretary or an assistant will of
course mark the record. Usually the former procedure will
be better. Certainly the marking of any kind of record in a
manner that involves the attention of the children at the beginning of the session is a very poor way of launching a
teaching situation.

The use of attendance records. The use which will be
made of these records of attendance may mean much in the
administrative program of the school. It is to be questioned
if "average attendance" reveals very much of what is really
happening. One department superintendent was heard to
say, "We simply must have a big attendance at Easter, for
our average for this year is way below what it was last year."
In other words, if a considerable number of children could
attend for only the one day, the record would look better;
but this is certainly a very superficial view of the work the
department is doing. If, however, the department has a
lower average attendance, week by week, it may mean that
absentees are not being carefully looked after, that the community is changing and the children must come from longer
distances, that the work of the department is not so effective,
the teachers are irregular in attendance, or the attitude of
the church toward its educational program is decreasing in
interest and effort.

Or it may even mean that the school has heretofore had a
larger attendance than its equipment and leadership could
support and it is now finding a normal level. But certainly
no church that has the rooms and leadership to teach a hun-

dred primary children should be satisfied if it has only fifty, or even ninety. And if its enrollment of primary children is one hundred and its average attendance is only sixty, something is wrong. Allowance for illness and other legitimate causes of absence should not bring the average attendance below 80 per cent of the enrollment. However, the emphasis on being present every Sunday should not be so emphatic and so reinforced by awards and the disapproval of every absence, that children (or adults, for that matter) who are ill with colds or other infectious sickness feel that they must attend the school at any cost.

There is another use of attendance records which may be of great value in determining administrative methods. That is the study of individual attendance records. One department made a list of the children who had been present every Sunday during the year, those who had been present fifty Sundays, those present between forty and fifty and so on down the list. To discover that in a department of fifty children there were only fifteen who had been present more than forty Sundays, and there were twenty-five children who had been present fewer than fifteen Sundays, was a revelation.

The next step when discoveries of this sort have been made is to find the cause. The leaders in this particular department were obliged to reach the conclusion that the high percentage of absence was due to the fact that the parents did not consider the work of the church school of sufficient importance to sacrifice Sunday visits and their own convenience in order to make it possible for their children to attend regularly. Under the guidance of the education committee and in cooperation with a committee of parents who really cared about the success of the church school, the church carried out plans by which the parents learned more of the objectives of its educational program and the importance of having their children present regularly.

Looking after absentees. Under normal conditions the teacher's personal contact with the home will be sufficient to take care of this important matter. If the teacher really cares about the members of her group and is interested in them, it is not a matter of administrative routine to look after them when they are absent but an expression of genuine and friendly interest. If through any unusual circumstances it is impossible for the teacher to get in touch with the absentees, the department superintendent or some other officer should do so. At this point the Parents' Committee may be of great assistance. The teacher should enter the cause for the absence in her records. If for any reason she has not been able to discover the cause, the department superintendent will wish to investigate. Local conditions make it necessary to vary the procedure. In one department there was an assistant who served as a hostess on Sunday morning, and who, because of having a large amount of leisure time, looked after the absentees. But nothing can take the place of first-hand knowledge of the child's home situation on the part of both teacher and department superintendent. One can work intelligently with a group of children only when they are known as individuals and this would, of course, involve a knowledge of their home background.

Record of the child's achievement. There is a third form of record which is not so universally kept. A personal record of the children's attainments in Christian living may be used to guide the teacher and other leaders in building their program and selecting materials that would provide the children with the opportunities for experiences they evidently need. A narrative of each child's growth may include incidents that reveal his attitudes, indicate changes and needs. Such a record may be only an outline in the form of notes made after each session, or it may be in story form. Such a record should always be appreciative in its tone. It may include information about illnesses, physical conditions discovered. Records of this kind help to keep the children before the teacher's eyes and should be studied when teaching plans are made.

ORDERING SUPPLIES AND WORK MATERIALS

In some church schools there is a budget allowance for each department. The department superintendent is asked to confer with her co-workers and to present a statement as to the probable needs. This allowance is then made in the budget and all materials must be purchased out of that sum. In other schools there is a purchasing agent for the entire school and everything is ordered through that person. In any case, it is desirable that there shall be one person in each department through whom the requests for working materials shall be cleared. There is economy in purchasing paper, picture mounts, poster sheets, pencils, crayolas, paste, and other working materials in quantity, provided there is a place in which these may be kept clean and accounted for.

The ordering of the supplies which accompany the course of study used in the department should be cared for long enough in advance to make sure that these materials are in the hands of the teachers in ample time. Duplicate copies of the order blanks sent to the school should be secured so that the department superintendent and her teachers may see this and know the complete list of materials available. Frequently these items do not mean anything to the general officer who orders the supplies, but are very important to the teachers and leaders. In one case, the teachers found themselves at a disadvantage because they did not have certain pictures that were referred to in connection with their lesson materials. They had not requested them because they did not know they were available and it occasioned considerable delay to order them after the discovery was made. Teachers' textbooks or quarterlies, pupils' books or leaflets, picture sets, and story papers usually constitute the supplies which are prepared by the publisher. In addition, there should be reference books, pictures secured from other sources, songbooks for the leader and the accompanist, reading books for the children and a few copies of the Bible in large print. It is the business of the department superintendent to see that teachers and children are supplied with the materials and sources that they need to carry on their work.

The teacher should have copies of the lesson materials which are provided for the children and should receive these at the beginning of the quarter. The books which are provided for home use as part of many lesson courses should be as familiar to the leaders as to the children and their parents. The responsibility for seeing that these books reach the home is shared by the department superintendent and teachers. The appreciation which the leaders show for these books will be reflected in the children's attitude. If the pupils' material is in leaflet form, waste will be avoided if at the beginning of each quarter the complete set of papers for each child is assembled and placed in a manila envelope which bears his name. The envelopes for the children of a group may be kept together in one place, ready for their use at the proper time. If a child is absent, he receives the folder, either by mail or when he returns.

ADMINISTRATIVE RELATIONSHIPS

Inter-group activities. It is through the department superintendent that inter-group activities may be carried forward. This does not mean that two classes or groups of children with their teachers cannot spontaneously enter into a common enterprise. Usually, however, there will be less likelihood of waste of time or enthusiasm if the department superintendent can help to clear the way for the joint activity. Sometimes it will involve the cooperation of the entire department as when one group asks the others to join in learning or singing a new song or in carrying out some project which requires the help of all. Perhaps the first intimation which the department superintendent has is a request from a group of children. Sometimes the teacher of the group will have let her know in advance that such a request may come. Particularly when the activities involve other departments of the church life, the department superintendent will help to establish the connections that are necessary.

Visitors. Sometimes the visitors have come to observe the work of the department, perhaps in connection with a training course they are taking or to get inspiration for their own work. Sometimes the visitor is a friend or relative of one of the children. The amount of information which will be made available to the visitor will depend upon the purpose in coming. But in any case, a visitor is a delightful opportunity for practicing the courtesy and friendliness which are part of Christian living. One group of children made a book which would tell visitors something about their program, the songs they sang, the work they did and the plan of their department. Committees of children planned for their comfort and happiness. Of course visitors will not be asked to "talk to the children," unless it has been arranged in advance and they are known to have a suitable message. There are not usually as many visitors in a Primary Department as in those for the younger children, and the problem of the visitor who laughs or makes comments and in other ways fails to enter into the spirit of the department, is not as acute, but it is sometimes necessary to make a definite effort to overcome such a tendency. One department had a very attractive folder which was given to each visitor and in which the spirit of worship and fellowship was expressed in a simple statement concerning the work of the department. Certain suggestions as to the way in which they might get the most satisfaction out of visiting the department were also made. Someone was ready to accompany them on a tour of the department. Such procedures as these are necessary when there are a large number of visitors who come to observe the school.

Relation to the education committee. This committee or board is the one responsible for the whole educational task of the church. Its name and membership vary in different denominations and local churches. Usually it is appointed by the officials of the church and responsible to the church through them. In some instances the primary superintendent is a member of the education committee or board. In others, there is a representative for the entire Children's Division, through whom the primary workers make known their problems and requests to the committee. Sometimes there is no direct representation of the age-group leaders in the local school. In this case it would be necessary for the primary superintendent to confer with the general superintendent, or possibly with some designated member of the committee, concerning the problems in which the guidance of the education committee is needed.

Perhaps the program of the school is administered through a council or workers' conference, in which case the department superintendent will cooperate in the entire program of the church and lead her staff of teachers and officers into this cooperative relationship.

If there is a chairman or director or supervisor of children's work, the primary superintendent will probably be the member on the committee or staff to counsel concerning the work of the Primary Department and to share in planning the total program of children's work.

It is of the greatest importance that a cordial attitude shall exist between the workers in the various departments. When the leaders in one department lack appreciation for the work being done in another, the unity of the educational program is marred and its effectiveness decreased. Children are very sensitive to attitudes of this kind and develop unfriendly feelings as a result.

When there is more than one leader of the primary work in the church, the education committee or some other recognized agency should make it possible for these leaders to work together in the building of a complete program for primary children. When the church cooperates in community vacation or weekday schools the way should be opened for the cooperation of the children's leaders in these several agencies. Frequently the school or church is represented by someone in an administrative capacity, but no provision is made for the integration of the various programs. The primary superintendent of the church must be ready and eager to enter into such conferences and relationships as will insure a complete and unified religious experience for the children.

THE QUALITY OF LEADERSHIP

The workers in the Primary Department must be able to work with each other, with parents, and with other leaders in the church. The very essence of Christian personality will find expression in, and be tested by, these relationships. Children are sensitive to the slightest evidence of discord and the spiritual climate of the department is destroyed by it.

The workers in the department must believe in children. They must have respect for their personalities. They must know how to guide without dominating and to accept graciously changes in plans.

The department superintendent and the staff must be the sort of people who are not made nervous by the buzzing activities of children. There is a vast difference between the noise and confusion of running about for the sake of mere activity and the noise that naturally accompanies purposeful activity.

Children measure up to responsibility when it is not beyond their capacity and they can be relied upon to do a great many things in which judgment, originality, and real perseverance are required. A superintendent who was leading her department to make the transition from the stiff and rigid program which centered in the leader to a more informal and natural one said, "I am continually surprised by what good sense the children have!"

SUGGESTIONS FOR FURTHER STUDY AND DISCUSSION

1. Make a complete analysis of the administration in the Primary Department. Indicate in which items the children should share and what value the experience would have for them.

2. The Primary Department was assembled for worship. The department superintendent was in charge. Two teachers remained at the back of the room near the supply cabinet. One of them was getting out the pictures she would need that day. They were having a conversation in low tones. Why do you think they did this, and how would you go about changing their attitude?

3. If a new child, very shy, came to the Primary Department, how would you proceed with enrolling and placing him in a class?

4. Prepare a list of ways in which the department superintendent can work with the teachers, and the teachers with the superintendent. Or, in the case of the department unit plan of organization, the ways in which the superintendent-teachers and the assistants work together.

5. Outline the duties of a department secretary. The pianist.

6. Plan a small booklet that would help an adult visitor to fit into the situation and understand the work of a department or group.

Chapter X

PLANNING FOR IMPROVEMENT

PRELIMINARY OBSERVATION

1. Recall your first experience in teaching. What help did you receive from the department superintendent or other church school leader?

2. Talk with a new or prospective teacher and discover what she would like to have by way of preparation or preliminary help.

3. Make a list of the conditions that should be improved in a Primary Department you know. How could the leaders and teachers decide upon and carry on a process of improvement?

The Christian nurture of primary children in the church requires that the highest ideals shall be held by all the workers engaged in it. It naturally follows that they can never be quite satisfied with the results they can see or the conditions under which they work. To be satisfied would probably mean that the ideals were not high enough.

A teacher in a training school for public school teachers would often say to them, "Whatever failure comes, the fault is within." This seemed unfair in some situations. What she wanted them to see was not only that one must always take the conditions into account in one's plans and work, but that the place to begin to make improvements is within oneself. The habit of looking within for the cause of failure need not lead to discouragement. There is reason for great encouragement, because with God's help one can change what one finds there.

When children are inattentive (which means attentive to something else more interesting), or unresponsive, or when plans for a session do not work out satisfactorily, it is so easy to say, "Our room is so badly arranged," or "We have so many interruptions," or "The home does not make children feel the importance of church school," or "That Brown boy disrupts everything!" But to ask oneself, "What did I fail to do that I should have done?" or "What mistake did I make in what I did or the way I did it?" gets at the root of the problem. Of course one should do something to change the room arrangement, remove the causes of interruptions or the opportunity for them; and parents should be given the fullest information about the work of the church and have a share in it; and the Brown boy should be given an opportunity to feel that he is part of the life of the department and responsible for its success. But while all those desirable changes are coming about (and they will probably take some time in the doing) the leader must take all of the probable hindrances into account and find ways of improving what she does and the way she does it. From that point of beginning within, the improvement of conditions can go forward with the greatest assurance of success.

One thing is certain, improvement comes only through planning, and planning requires careful thinking, time, patience, and the wisdom which God gives to those who seek it.

THE IMPROVEMENT OF WORKERS

No improvement is possible unless there is a sense of need. The more specific the awareness, the easier it is to meet the need. Sometimes a worker will become conscious of need at a certain point in the process of teaching and will say, "I wish I knew more about—" but is not sure how to find the help needed, or feels too limited in time or strength to avail herself of the resources available. Or it may be that a child's question opens up a whole field of knowledge which the teacher has not explored.

The fellowship among the workers in a department should be such that it is easy to talk frankly about the need for improving one's knowledge and skill or for finding richer resources in religion. To be on the defensive, finding excuses, deprives one of the help which comes from the experiences of working together.

In religious experience. All experiences may be religious if they are enriched and motivated by the spirit of God. There are certain specific experiences of prayer and meditation of which teachers stand in very special need. The idea that "spiritual mindedness" and practical working can rarely be found in the same person is certainly not true of a teacher of children, if indeed it ever is. All Christians need to grow in their ability to use the resources of prayer and other experiences of worship. No one should be ashamed to confess need of help in this aspect of the Christian life. There are books for use in private prayer and meditation which are of great value. There are books about prayer which will open up new spiritual resources.[1] The hymnal of the church should be familiar to the teacher, not for use with primary children, but for personal enrichment. Bible study for one's own help and inspiration should not be crowded out by the use of the Bible in teaching children.

A group of teachers might well devote part of the time of their conferences to conversation about this important part of their own growth. It is only persons who themselves find deep meaning in worship who can worship with children.

It may be in their own basic religious ideas that teachers feel the greatest need. Unless their concept of God is clear and Christian they will feel insecure both as persons and as teachers of children. Helpful books on the great truths of religion, especially the nature of God,[2] should be available to all teachers. The minister will usually be able to help either through personal interviews or by coming to a conference of the workers in a department. There may be other religious leaders in a community who could be helpful in this way. Sitting down together for a conversation on basic religious ideas can be a rich spiritual experience and lead to growth in Christian thought and life. Workers with children are often cut off from some of the enriching influences which come to other adults in the church. The program of leadership education in the church as well as such informal contacts should help this situation.

In Bible knowledge. Graded lesson materials provide considerable Bible background in connection with the teachers' materials. These take advantage of the best information to be found in commentaries and other reference books. Moreover they all require the teacher's use of the Bible, instead of printing small sections of it. But teachers need to know much more than they will use in teaching children. Bible courses in leadership classes offer excellent opportunities for increasing Bible knowledge. Sometimes children's workers take leadership courses year after year, dealing with their own department but do not avail themselves of the excellent general

---

[1] *Prayer and the Common Life,* by Georgia Harkness is one of many books.

[2] *The Will of God,* by Leslie D. Weatherhead, is typical of such books.

courses on the Bible. It is true, these courses will probably not deal with ways in which the Bible is to be used with children but teachers need to enrich their knowledge of the Old and New Testaments for themselves and as a basis for their use of lesson materials. There are also books which help in personal Bible reading.[3]

In knowledge of children. A never ending field of study is found in children themselves and in books about them. The teacher of children must be continually observing, interpreting what is discovered, and making use of this growing knowledge in living and working with children. Books will help[4] and will give more meaning to what is observed in child-life. A simple record of what is known about each child will be helpful and provide a way of sharing this information with others who work with him. The teachers' understanding and sympathy should grow as her knowledge of particular children increases.

In personal enrichment. Everything which enriches the life of a teacher improves his teaching, if only by giving new enthusiasm to his attitudes toward life. The primary worker who did everything well but from a serious sense of duty, felt a new insight into truth and beauty when she first learned to enjoy a symphony. Sometimes visits to an art gallery or the enjoyment of prints of great paintings, or reading poetry, or the cultivation of new friendships, will bring joy and satisfaction in living and be reflected in the personality. A group of primary teachers might well share their experiences of this kind and stimulate each other to make new discoveries. A successful teacher must first of all be a successful person.

IMPROVEMENT OF TEACHING

An important part of the responsibility of the primary superintendent of leading teacher is that of helping the workers to grow in their ability to teach. This is usually done through supervision, which may take a variety of forms. It is essential that the superintendent shall be conscious of this part of her work as well as the administrative duties. Teachers have a

---

[3] *A Guide to Understanding the Bible*, by Harry Emerson Fosdick is a stimulating book and will lead to new insights.

[4] *The Children We Teach*, by Elizabeth S. Whitehouse, *Faith of Our Children*, by Mary Alice Jones, *Understanding Children*, by Lewis J. Sherrill, are helpful and practical.

right to the help in their work which can come only through
some form of supervision, which may be defined as a cooperative effort on the part of a group of people, under leadership,
to discover the points at which the work they are doing may
be improved and to set up procedures through which this
improvement may be brought about.

The approach to supervision. Unless there is a sense of
need there will not be an enthusiastic desire for improvement.
Sometimes that feeling of need is very vague and needs to be
brought to a focus by some specific situation. Perhaps the
teachers and leaders have attended the classes of a training
school and have become aware of certain weaknesses in their
work. Or it may be that only one or two in the group have
had this experience. There are different ways of reacting to
new ideas. The teacher may become discouraged and want to
give up her work. Or, that may be a defensive attitude in
which the discouraged worker is unconsciously trying to secure
consolation, the assurance that she is doing good work and
the insistence that she shall continue, without having to pay
the price of further study and harder work. Or these teachers
with new ideals may be very enthusiastic and ready to begin
all sorts of new things, without having a very definite idea as
to what should be done next. Sometimes new ideals result in
a critical attitude toward the other workers in the department
and the conditions under which the work must be done. It
is not unusual to find a trained worker who has become out of
sympathy with the work in her local church. This would
seem to indicate a very imperfect kind of training and a mis-
directed one, or personal limitations in the individual. There
are very few conditions that cannot be improved if one is wise
and tactful.

Yet out of all or any of these situations a fine program for
the improvement of the work in any department may emerge
if a leader with vision is ready to take advantage of them.

Through conferences of workers. When needs have been
felt, even vaguely or when particular problems arise, in any
of the ways indicated above, any steps to bring about changes
must begin with common understanding and ideals. This
can usually be brought about through frank and purposeful
conference. Perhaps this will be the regular conference of the
department leaders and teachers or it may be a special conference called to face a particular problem.

Sometimes the need that has been felt is a superficial one or is merely the evidence of something much deeper and more fundamental. It is the problem of the leader to direct the conference so that the basic needs will be discovered and recognized. For example, several teachers in a Primary Department were disturbed because the children did not sing. One of them felt it was because the songs were not tuneful enough or the kind that children like. Another teacher, who was a musician, felt that the method of teaching songs was at fault. It would have been easily possible for the department superintendent to feel that these criticisms were personal and to have taken offense. She had the good sense to do nothing of the kind but said instead, "I agree with you, there is something wrong with the singing in our department. Can we talk it over at our conference?"

The department superintendent launched the discussion by asking, "When children do not enter heartily into singing, what may be the reasons for it?" Then she listed on the blackboard all of the possible reasons suggested by the teachers and in a few instances by herself. Such reasons as the children's interest, their singing ability, kind of songs to which they were accustomed, and others, were discussed. Finally they arrived at the statement of the problem in this form, "What is the purpose of singing in the Primary Department?" and it was agreed that through observation, reading and thought, they would prepare themselves to discuss the problem at their next meeting. The result was that they entered upon a study of children's worship, the place of music in worship, and of the experiences that lead children to desire to worship. The improvement in the children's singing was only one of many changes that came about because of the discovery and analysis of a particular problem.

Through the acceptance of objectives. It may be that the education committee has adopted or set up certain objectives for the whole church school, which in turn will need to be interpreted in terms of the experiences of the children, young people or adults in each of the departments. The study of these objectives, the interpretation of them for their own work, will serve as an approach to a program for the improvement in their work.

But the mere acceptance of a set of objectives will mean

very little unless the group of workers themselves pass through
something of the same experiences as resulted in the setting
up of the objectives. Of course it would not be possible for
the workers in every local church to do all of the research and
engage in all of the investigations that have led to the development of such a list of objectives as those adopted by the International Council of Religious Education.[5] But unless the
teachers and leaders who are attempting to achieve these objectives understand something of the reasons underlying them,
the objectives lack inspiration and meaning.

It would be interesting for a group of teachers and leaders
in a Primary Department to make their own list of objectives
and then compare them with such a list as the one that has
been mentioned. Back of the statement of objectives or the
acceptance of them, there must be a knowledge of the children and their needs and an appreciation of their capacity for
Christian living.

Through visiting the teacher at work. When the teachers
and leaders of a department have agreed upon the need for
improvement and are ready to take steps to achieve it, there
are various practical procedures that may be used.

The department superintendent may arrange to visit the
class group and observe its work. She should arrive at the
very beginning of the period and remain through until the
end, if it is at all possible to do so. Whether or not she will
participate in the work of the group depends upon the plan
agreed upon by the superintendent and the teacher in advance
of the session. Perhaps she will be freest to observe everything
that takes place if she sits with the group or at the edge of it
and quietly observes. If any notes are taken, it should be done
in such an inconspicuous way that neither the children nor the
teacher will be conscious of it. Probably it would be better if
no notes were taken at the time but the description of the
teaching period written out fully as soon as possible after the
visit.

Within a short time the superintendent and the teacher
should have a conference and go over together everything
that happened in the teaching period, noting all of the evidences of success as well as those that indicate failure. If
the superintendent will avoid all appearance of setting up her

---

[5]May be secured from many denominational offices.

own judgment as final and will help the teacher herself to discover the weaknessess of the procedure and the possible changes that might be made, the result from the visit will be more satisfactory.

During this conference, plans should be made for another teaching period. Perhaps the plans will include such items as: (1) probable experiences and needs of the children; (2) specific objectives or desired outcome for the teaching period; (3) activities and other teaching procedures that would provide the children with the greatest opportunity for learning; (4) materials which would probably be used during the teaching period. The plans should make ample provision for adaptation to meet the situations that arise, but should also give the teacher a sense of readiness to meet the occasion. Perhaps the superintendent will visit a second time and they will again confer on the result and make plans for the future. It may be found that there are conditions unfavorable to good work, such as lack of light, poor ventilation, crowded conditions, lack of equipment. Plans for improving these conditions, as well as making the best of what is available, will be made. The teacher may also discover that she lacks certain skill such as the ability to stimulate and guide the children's discussion in such a way that the interest of the children is maintained. Plans for study and practice will be made.

Pre-teaching and post-teaching interviews. Frequently the best procedure is for the department superintendent to arrange for an interview with each teacher in the department to consider the needs of the children in that particular group, the objectives for which the teacher should be working, the methods and materials which the teacher may use. The interview centers in a plan for a particular session. When the teacher makes a plan and notes carefully what takes place with a view of discussing it later, the whole planning and teaching experience becomes vitalized and takes on the character of an adventure.

As soon as possible after the teaching session which grew out of the plans made in the pre-teaching interview, the teacher and the superintendent meet and discuss what took place in the class session. It will require tact and a very impersonal attitude to avoid the impression of criticism on the part of the superintendent and defense on the part of the teacher. A due proportion of rejoicing in success and analyzing failures should be preserved. It may not be possible in the first interview or two to get at the real root of the difficulty. Perhaps in the beginning the teacher needs encouragement and is not yet ready to recognize all her failures and the causes for them. This will come gradually as she continues to plan, to check results and to plan again.

There may be teachers in the department who, no matter how tactfully the matter is approached, would resent having an interview of this kind. This attitude in itself indicates a fear of criticism and of being found wanting. Yet the teacher may be a good one in some respects and there may be many reasons why it is desirable to retain her. Usually the best plan is to proceed with those teachers who are anxious to improve and who welcome the opportunity for receiving assistance in their planning. Frequently the improvements in the class group where the teachers have been cooperative in these methods of supervision have been so marked that the other teachers have discovered their inadequacy and have sought the assistance of conference and interviews.

Through reading. When the superintendent and the teacher have discovered improvements that may be undertaken, wisely directed reading may often be one of the first steps. It is usually best to suggest definite pages or a chapter, rather than an entire book, unless the teacher is an experienced student. Sometimes all that will be necessary is to indicate various sources and let the teacher browse. Helpful articles which one discovers are usually read with more enthusiasm than those which one is requested to read. Yet sometimes the teacher may be saved a great deal of time if the superintendent will indicate specific places where help will probably be found. A file of religious education magazines, especially those containing help for children's workers, a reading library that is kept fresh and up to date, source books in which the teachers may find both materials and suggested procedures, clippings kept in some sort of file or scrapbooks, all prove valuable in providing helpful reading for a staff of teachers. It is better to begin with a very small amount of such material constantly in use and circulation than to wait until it is possible to have a large and well-balanced library.

One department superintendent arranged a small office in a corner of the room. She had there a desk, a bookcase, a file, and a bulletin board. Sometime during the session every teacher found it possible to go to that corner and usually something interesting was to be found there. It was the place where the department superintendent interviewed children and parents and other visitors. It made the task of supervision simpler and avoided the bad practice of making the table at the front of the room, which is frequently the worship center, the place where the department superintendent kept her materials and centered her activity.

Through standards for teachers. "What shall I say to the prospective teacher whom I am inviting to join the staff of the Primary Department?" was a question which had puzzled a certain superintendent and which she brought to the teachers in one of their conferences. Out of their discussion grew a very simple standard which they accepted for themselves and which the superintendent might use in her conferences with prospective teachers. It included what the teachers considered the minimum requirements, such as, "Spend at least one hour a week in preparation," "Be present not less than ten minutes in advance of the session" (a longer period would be desirable in both of these cases), "Have some weekday contact with the children in their homes," "Take at least one leadership training course each year," "Read one book or magazine each year." The value was not in the standard itself so much as in the fact that the teachers made it and accepted it and that it opened the door for the improvement of the work through reading and preparation.

Through use of a self-rating scale. It is not wholesome for teachers to be too much given to introspection and yet there are certain questions of personality and preparation which no one but the individual himself can face fully. The use of a self-rating scale has been found valuable in guiding this self-inspection so that it does not become morbid. Only as the use of such a rating scale leads to a plan for improvement, has it any value.

As in the case of the standards just referred to, a group of teachers may prepare their own rating scale. The discussion that would lead to the preparation of such a scale would be quite as profitable as the use of it when it had been made.

Or, the group of teachers and leaders may prefer to examine rating scales that have been made by others and either adopt one of these or modify it for their use.

Rating scales such as these may be purely personal matters so far as the teacher's use of them is concerned. That is, the teacher may privately score herself and in conference with the department superintendent work out a program for her own improvement. Of course, the general attitude of the teacher will enter into the way in which she scores herself. An undue amount of humility, just as much as too much self-assurance, will make the scoring inaccurate. A conference of the leaders and teachers in the department before they use the self-rating scale, when the matter is approached in a frank but impersonal way, will be helpful. If the attitude of seeking the truth and working out a basis for improvement can be developed, the process of self-rating may be a very helpful one. Of course the result of the scoring will be entirely confidential and no comparisons will ever be possible.

Leadership training. There are available through community training schools, denominational training schools for periods of one or two weeks, summer training schools, laboratory schools, correspondence courses and other channels, many opportunities for securing additional training in the teaching of religion. Of all forms of training the laboratory school is most effective since students have an opportunity to practice under the guidance of experienced teachers. The teacher who discovers her own need of some particular skill, or who tastes the joy of success in working with children, is always eager for additional training.

A young woman in a certain church was asked to take one of the grades in the Primary Department. Her general education and culture were very good, but she had had no specific training for this particular task. Before she would give her answer she asked, "What training do you make available to people who are to do work of this kind?" The form in which she asked this question is in itself a challenge to the church. It has no right to ask people to assume responsibilities as grave and important as the teaching of children without making available to them the training that is necessary. It may not be able to do this alone, but in cooperation with other churches in the community or in its own denomination it should be able to arrange for leadership training classes for all its leaders and teachers. While diplomas may be secured and various stages of training marked by achievements, it is in reality a process that goes on indefinitely, for ideals of education grow and courses of training change. It is doubtful if one can ever claim to be a "trained" teacher, one is always "in training."

Previews of teaching materials. Some phases of supervision will center in very specific problems such as those that arise in connection with the lesson courses being used in the department. In its broadest sense, curriculum includes everything that enters into the department. The materials of worship, the activities of the department, are all part of the curriculum. An exceedingly important part of the curriculum consists of the lesson materials which the school provides for the use of its teachers and children. Certainly in no phase of religious education has there been greater change and improvement than in the lesson courses. There is an increasing effort on the part of writers and editors to provide material that actually centers in the experiences of the children and provides them an opportunity for Christian living and learning. The more closely lesson material is related to the experiences of the children, the more surely will the teacher have to know how to select the materials and activities which meet the needs and are related to the problems of her group of children. This means that lesson material is more flexible and informal in its character.

It is a good plan for the department superintendent to sit down with individual teachers, with the teachers of one grade, or with all the teachers of the department, and give careful attention to the lesson materials which are presented for their use. To read and discuss the Foreword in the teacher's book, to discover and discuss the specific objectives or desired outcomes, to find what experiences of the children are included in the materials and whether or not those are actual experiences of the children in your own group, are all procedures that will lead to a better understanding of the materials and methods which are available for the teacher. Usually there is much more material suggested than can be used in the time available. This is provided so that the teacher may select that which meets the needs of her own group.

The leader should help the teacher review the course of study, expand or change it to meet situations, and integrate the work of all the groups, where such integration is desirable for both the larger and the smaller groups. Sometimes an adaptation of the work of a group will be made when a major departmental activity has grown out of solving some pressing problem or meeting a need.

Sometimes the department superintendent will also have the opportunity to co-operate with the education committee in the selection of lesson courses, and in the addition of other source materials. Certainly the choice of the course study is an exceedingly important one and while we will keep in mind that our curriculum is not material-centered, we must also remember that good materials are necessary.

If teachers in the church school could get away from the limitations of "next Sunday's lesson" and see the whole scope of the plan, they would find greater satisfaction in the use of the material. Sometimes it is possible to readjust the material so that it will come at a time when it is more suitable for the children. If the lesson course will be looked upon as source material rather than a schedule to be slavishly followed, if the teachers are alert to the real needs of their group and if careful supervision is given by the department superintendent, the lesson courses will be of much greater value to teachers and children.

IMPROVEMENT OF CONDITIONS

The teachers, officers, children and their relations with each other, are the most important factors in the work of the department. But rooms, equipment, time schedules, working materials, are important too and any plans for improvement must deal with them. A study of conditions and a list of improvements which are needed should be made at frequent intervals. Some of the changes may be made immediately and others may call for long-term planning. Many of them will come about gradually through the improvement of work in progress and through conference.

Regular department conferences. No matter how fine the spirit of cooperation may be, nor how willing the group of workers may be to follow the leadership of the superintendent, this spirit can only operate when it is based upon shared ideals.

The necessity for attending a workers' conference at least once a month should be understood and accepted by anyone coming into the Primary Department as a teacher, assistant, or officer, as certainly as the responsibility for being present at every session of the department.

A conference of forty-five minutes, or even one hour, held before or after some other meeting, is not adequate. At least an hour and a half, not less often than once a month should be looked upon as a minimum. When some situation needs special attention, such as a change in the schedule of the session, the problems connected with new lesson materials, may require additional conference. Some groups of workers, when facing these and similar problems, have found it necessary to meet once a week for a period of two or three months. In fact, there are departments in which a weekly meeting is held regularly and it is not surprising that they are very successful.

The frequency of conferences will depend upon the number of preview and pre-teaching conferences which are planned. When these are held as suggested earlier in this chapter or according to some similar plan, the department conferences may be held less frequently, but they should be regularly scheduled so that busy workers can plan to attend.

There are many factors in the situation which must be considered in deciding when the meeting shall be held, such as the distances the workers must come, the transportation, whether they are employed or at home, the plan of the church for general workers' conferences or committees.

There may be a monthly workers' conference with the departments meeting before or after. For the sake of the good morale of the whole school, it is desirable that the primary staff shall be in this general workers' conference. There are two dangers that must be avoided, that the time for the department conference may be too short and that the members may be too tired to give their best thought to the important matters that must be considered. When the workers are employed during the day, come to the church for supper (or go home and come later to the church), spend an hour in a department conference and another hour in a general conference, the school spirit may be fostered by this gathering of all the workers but certainly no very thorough discussion of educational principles or procedures in the department can be possible. However, if this is the only time available, careful planning can make it profitable to a certain extent.

In one church where transportation made week-night meetings difficult, the conferences were held on the first Sunday afternoon of each month, the department conferences at four, or as much earlier as the staff of any department might wish, the general conference at five-fifteen, and a light supper was served at six, followed by the young people's meetings and preaching service. This arrangement made it possible for the department conferences to be as long as any group wished, even including occasionally a luncheon at noon with the whole afternoon for conference.

If the primary workers are not employed, a morning or afternoon conference will have the advantage of freedom from hurry or fatigue. Provision should also be made for contact with the workers in the other departments of the school, and in the general workers' conference.

If the department is organized on a single grade basis, probably the best plan is to have bi-monthly conferences of the workers in all grades. Also, when the staff is large or when the problems under consideration relate particularly to curriculum and class procedures, it may be more desirable to have the conferences by grades, with provision for a sufficient number of department conferences to preserve the unity of the work.

The program of the department conference should include spiritual enrichment through prayer, a passage from the Bible in which new meaning is found because of its relation to the work in hand, a beautiful poem or picture study. A leader of children who feels that she must go outside the work she is doing to find inspiration for her own soul, is evidently not finding the fellowship and joy that may come to a group of workers who face their task together reverently. New teachers who are coming into the department and who have not yet found themselves in the work they are doing often get just the perspective that they need by joining with the other members of the staff in occasions of worship and fellowship.

There may be a discussion of some subject of significance for the Christian education of primary children. Perhaps this will be the review of a book or of an article. The educational magazines of several denominations and the International Journal of Religious Education contain many articles which are excellent for just this purpose. Reports from training classes or from a laboratory school will also stimulate discussion.

The department program and schedule and class procedure should be discussed. This may be in the form of reports made by the department superintendent and teachers, to be discussed by the whole group, or it may be that changes in schedule, new material for the program, and new lesson courses are to be discussed.

A program of improvement. In order that the new ideas and ideals that are stimulated by the department conference shall not be lost, it is a good plan to have a small committee on recommendation who will be alert to the discussion and prepare to formulate and bring into the next meeting certain concrete recommendations concerning the improvement of their own department. Recommendations may grow out of particular needs and emergencies in the department itself, as well as out of the discussion of educational principles. These recommendations may include the objectives which the group originate or accept as the goal of their work. Some of these recommendations would of necessity go to the Education Committee for final approval, and some of them may come to the department conference from the Education Committee. Many of the recommendations will relate to work within the department and will be carried out by the teachers and officers. Improvements in room arrangements, in the use of equipment and working materials, in the order of the department program, and in methods of work should grow out of conference and agreement among workers. Plans for future and more far-reaching changes should take definite form in recommendations even though they cannot be carried out for some time to come. They may be changed in the meantime as the ideals of the workers grow through experience and training.

OPPORTUNITY FOR OUTSIDE CONTACTS

With public school teachers. It has been found very helpful to have as the guest of the Primary workers' conference, the teachers for the first three grades of the public school, especially from those school buildings attended by the children of the Primary Department. This may be a meeting for fellowship and exchange of information concerning objectives and procedures. It may be an occasion when the teachers in the Primary Department may raise certain problems which require information outside the church school teacher's contact. It may be best to have only one of the public school teachers at each meeting in order to make the inquires and discussions particularly practical.

With leaders in child welfare work. In cities and communities where various kinds of child welfare work are carried on, it is essential that the church school leader shall be informed about it. For each one to make individual investigation is a duplication of effort and in nearly every instance these leaders will welcome an opportunity to meet and talk with a group of children's teachers. Sometimes the eyes of the church school workers will be opened to conditions among their own children, of which they had been entirely unaware. Sometimes they will discover an avenue of service into which they may lead the children. In one instance a child clinic was opened in the church and a valuable health service made available to children and parents. In another instance the children became interested in supporting such a clinic and a milk station in another community.

Doctors and nurses, juvenile court officers, specialists in child psychology are all persons who can be of great value to church school teachers of children and will usually welcome the opportunity to have conference with them. It will be to the advantage of everyone if parents are also invited to these meetings and occasionally there may be combined conferences of the leaders in the different children's departments.

INTERDEPARTMENT CONFERENCES

The dangers of such complete departmentalization that the workers and children in one department have no contact with those in another, have already been referred to in connection with other problems. There are certain points at which the work of the different departments merge and there is necessity for conference. It is desirable, that at least once a year all the leaders and teachers of the children's departments should have a joint conference when the workers in each department present its objectives, describe the way in which they are working, and perhaps make a statement concerning certain problems that they are facing. Such a meeting might logically come early in the school year, so that the basis for intelligent cooperation through the year might be made in the beginning.

If there is a chairman (or supervisor, or director) of Children's Work in the church there will be plans for regular meetings and clearances.

There are always interdepartment activities for which arrangements must be made, such as the puppet play which the juniors are preparing and to which they wish to invite the primary children, or the exhibit and dramatization to which the primary children would like to invite the juniors. These could probably be arranged informally between the superintendents and teachers of the different groups. But such friendly occasions and a happy arrangement for them are much more likely to be successful if there has been the opportunity for conference and for the sharing of ideals on the part of all leaders. Strange as it may seem, it is not at all uncommon to find in church schools workers in one department who do not even know the names of the department superintendent or many of the teachers in another department. Sometimes there is a lack of appreciation of the work of other departments.

In all plans for improvement the needs of children must be kept central. The changes in conditions, the improvement in teaching, the development of the workers, are good to the degree that they give children a better opportunity for growth in Christian personality now and lead on "to the measure of the stature of the fullness of Christ."

SUGGESTIONS FOR FURTHER STUDY AND DISCUSSION

1. Plan three interviews between a department superintendent and a new teacher; the first, a month before she begins her work; the second, the week before; the third, the week following.

2. In the case of teachers who have been teaching for some time and are sensitive and inclined to resent suggestion, how would you go about making the procedure impersonal and helpful?

3. If a teacher invited the department superintendent into her class to observe the teaching period, how could the experi-

ence be made most helpful to the teacher and to the general work of the department?

4. Prepare a program for a Primary Workers' Conference that you would consider practical in your own church.

5. Outline a series of ten educational topics that would serve as the basis for the discussion periods for a year of Primary Conference programs.

6. Outline a program of improvement for your own department.